FORT MANDAN, APRIL 7, 1805

The party are in excellent health and sperits, zealously attached to the enterprise, and anxious to proceed....

CAPTAIN MERIWETHER LEWIS

NOVEMBER 3, 1805

A Mountain which we Suppose to be Mt. Hood,
is S. 85° E about 47 miles distant from the mouth
of quick sand river. This Mt. is covered with Snow and
in the range of mountains which we have passed through
and is of a conical form but rugid.

CLARK

THE
LEWIS & CLARK
COOKBOOK

Historic Recipes

FROM THE CORPS OF DISCOVERY
& JEFFERSON'S AMERICA

LESLIE MANSFIELD

CELESTIAL ARTS
Berkeley · Toronto

The engravings throughout are reproduced from *The Animal Kingdom Illustrated, Volume I,* by S. G. Goodrich, published by A. J. Johnson, New York: 1872; and from *Johnson's New Natural History, Volume II,* by S. G. Goodrich, published by A. J. Johnson, New York: 1879. The color plates are reproduced from *Mammalia: Johnson's Household Book of Nature,* published by A. J. Johnson, New York: 1880; from *Freshwater Fishes* by William Houghton, published by William Mackenzie, Edinburgh & London: 1879; from *The Illustrated Book of Poultry* by Lewis Wright, published by Cassell, Petter, Galpin & Company, London, Paris & New York: 1886; from *Revue Horticole Journal D'Horticulture Pratique* by the authors of *Bon Jardiner,* Paris: 1873–1882; and from *The North American Sylva* by Thomas Nuttall, published by A. N. Hart, Philadelphia: 1855.

P.O. Box 7123
Berkeley, California 94707
www.tenspeed.com

Distributed in Australia by Simon and Schuster Australia, in Canada by Ten Speed Canada, in New Zealand by Southern Publishers Group, in South Africa by Real Books, in Southeast Asia by Berkeley Books, and in the United Kingdom and Europe by Airlift Book Company.

Book design by Star Type, Berkeley

Library of Congress Cataloging-in-Publication Data

First printing, 2002
Printed in China

Dedication

Dedicated in loving memory to my grandfathers
Edgar Herman Johnson and Leslie M. Whipple.

Acknowledgements

First and foremost I thank my husband Richard who devoted all his spare time to helping me. His name truly deserves to be on the title page. I also thank my father, Stewart Whipple, for giving me the idea for this book and my mother, Marcia Whipple, for teaching me the love of the kitchen.

Thanks to Phil Wood, who makes dreams come true. Thanks to JoAnn Deck. Special thanks go to my dearest friend and editor, Veronica Randall, whose talent and vision guided me through this, our thirteenth book together. To Victoria Randall, for her eagle eye and great dinner parties. To Linda Davis, for the superb design and layout of this book.

From the Lewis and Clark National Bicentennial Committee, I thank both Michelle Bussard and Diane Norton for their support throughout this project. From the Lewis and Clark College in Portland, Oregon I thank Doug Erickson, Head of Special Collections, for his assistance with the research material. I also thank Jeremy Skinner, Assistant Archivist, Watzek Library, Lewis and Clark College, for vetting our scholarship. Thanks to Karen Christenson of the Portland Art Museum for helping to secure the beautiful cover.

The producers and purveyors of many of the ingredients and supplies for this book were extremely important to its success. They gave me unparalleled access to the finest of materials and I look forward to becoming greater friends with all of them in the future.

Finally, I thank my darling nephew, Gage Whipple, for his adventurous spirit and unfailing acceptance of new and strange foods.

Table of Contents

Color Plates

RED DEER

Preface

JANUARY 18, 1803 ➤ The river Missouri, & the Indians inhabiting it, are not as well known as is rendered desireable by their connection . . . with us. . . . An intelligent officer with ten or twelve chosen men . . . might explore the whole . . . to the Western Ocean ➤ JEFFERSON
in a confidential message to Congress

Thus, the seed was planted for what would become in the spring of the following year the most celebrated, controversial, and profitable piece of trailblazing in American history.

Artfully vague with the details, Jefferson's request for authorization for a military reconnaissance into an enormous, virtually unknown, and potentially hostile wilderness carefully avoided the word "military" altogether. Instead, Jefferson wrote seductively about the "great supplies of furs & peltry" upon which the 16th, 17th, and 18th century exploration and economy of North America relied. Anxious to break the British Hudson's Bay Company stranglehold on the all-important fur trade, Jefferson sensed that the correct geopolitical move was to find the key that would unlock the door to the West. The discovery of a "northern passage," a set of navigable waterways by which the Eastern Seaboard could be united with the trade routes of the Pacific, had been his leading theory—and private passion—for nearly twenty years.

In fact, in 1786 while ambassador to France, Jefferson engaged John Ledyard to attempt a continental crossing from Europe by way of Russia, central Asia, and Siberia, over the Bering Sea into Canada, then southward along the western coastline before eventually turning inland and eastward to the Missouri River. Incredibly, Ledyard walked 3,000 miles into Siberia before he was apprehended by Catherine the Great's troops and escorted back to Europe under suspicion of spying.

Jefferson was undaunted. While secretary of state, he commissioned French émigré Andre Michaux to find a route across the continent, this time from the eastern states to the Missouri. Michaux managed to reach Kentucky before, in an ironic twist of history, he was unmasked as a real spy in the service of Edmond Charles Genêt, French ambassador to Washington.

By the time Jefferson attained the White House in 1801, war was in the wind between Britain and France, and Jefferson knew that Napoleon would need cash to pay for it. To this end, on April 30, 1803, Jefferson signed into effect a $15,000,000 purchase of the Louisiana Territory, at one stroke doubling the size of the United States. This gigantic parcel of land comprising some 500,000,000 acres had been recently ceded by Spain to France in 1800. Jefferson bought it for the bargain price, even by early 19th century rates of exchange, of three cents an acre.

The Louisiana Purchase encompassed the entire river drainage of the Mississippi stretching westward to the Rocky Mountains and extending from Canada south to the Gulf of Mexico. It presented a vast *terra incognita,* containing uncounted nations of Indians, trackless mountains and woodlands, endless unexplored prairies, and wild, uncharted waters. It was the unknown promise of this limitless landscape that had fueled the energy and imagination of the president for nearly two decades.

It was to his secretary and former Virginia neighbor Captain Meriwether Lewis that Jefferson turned to lead the enterprise that would forever alter the course of a nation. Lewis chose old friend and army comrade William Clark as his second in command. Their mission:

> JUNE 20, 1803 ⟶ to explore the Missouri River, and such principal streams of it, as, by its course and communication with the waters of the pacific Ocean, whether the Columbia, Oregon, Colrado, or any other river, may offer the most direct and practible water-communication across the continent for the purposes of commerce. ⟵ JEFFERSON

In addition, the men were charged with carrying out meticulous scientific observations and calculations with regard to the geography and geology of the country through which they passed. Also, the indigenous flora and fauna were to be observed, identified, recorded, and collected whenever possible. Prior to the expedition, the North American continent was mostly a mystery based on the usually vague and often fanciful reporting of Spanish soldiers. Above all, Lewis and Clark were charged with establishing peaceful relations with any native peoples they might encounter. Their mandate:

> JUNE 20, 1803 ⟶ In all your intercourse with the natives, treat them in the most friendly and conciliatory manner which their own conduct will admit; allay all jealousies as to the object of your journey; satisfy them of its innocence; make them acquainted with the position, extent character, peaceable and commercial dispositions of the United States; of our wish to be neighbourly; friendly, and useful to them. ⟵ JEFFERSON

Thus, not only was the venture a voyage across 7,689 miles of unmapped, unsettled wilderness, the Corps of Discovery was to be the first diplomatic mission sent forth and financed by the American government into the unknown. Although the final cost of the enterprise reached $38,722.25, Jefferson's original request was a very modest $2,500 which Congress granted on February 28, 1803.

Scrupulous consideration was given to the selection of the crew members, who were chosen for their skills as hunters, boatmen, carpenters, blacksmiths, and all-around frontiersmen. "Gentlemen's sons" in search of adventure were discouraged from applying. By the spring of 1803, a company of 30 men had been assembled:

1st Squad	2nd Squad	3rd Squad
Sergeant Nathaniel Pryor	Sergeant Charles Floyd	Sergant John Ordway
Privates:	(died August 18, 1804)	Privates:
George Gibson	Sergeant Patrick Gass (pro-	John Robertson*
Thomas Howard	moted to succeed Floyd)	William Bratton
George Shannon	Privates:	John Colter
John Shields	Hugh McNeal	Alexander Willard
John Collins	Rueben Fields	William Werner
Joseph Whitehouse	Joseph Fields	Silas Goodrich
Peter Wiser	John Thompson	John Potts
Hugh Hall	Richard Windsor	Baptiste Lepage (replaced
	Pierre Crusette	Newman at Fort Mandan)
	Robert Frazier	John Newman*
	Francis Labiches	Moses Reed*
	Richard Warvington*	*sent back by April 7, 1805

The Corps included Clark's slave York and two interpreters, George Drouillard and Toussaint Charbonneau, who with his Shoshone wife, Sacajawea, and their infant son, Jean Baptiste, joined the party at Fort Mandan.

The expedition was stocked with supplies deemed sufficient to last the foreseeable length of the mission and included an extensive inventory of trading goods for use as gifts for the Indian tribes, as well as the latest in scientific instruments and equipment. Records show that Captain Lewis requested 200 pounds of the "Best Rifle Powder" and 400 pounds of lead. The lead was ingeniously formed into watertight containers into which the gunpowder was stored and sealed. When the gunpowder ran out, the lead containers could be melted down and molded into shot.

The following provisions are listed in Clark's Journals and offer a fascinating glimpse of early 19th century essential comestibles:

15 bags of parched meal, 9 bags of common meal, 11 bags hulled corn, 30 half barrels of flour, 2 bags of flour, 7 bags of biscuit, 4 barrels of biscuit, 7 barrels of salt, 50 kegs of Pork, 2 boxes of candles, 1 bag of candle-wick, 1 bag of coffee, 1 bag of Beens, 1 bag of pees, 2 bags of sugar, 1 keg of Hogs lard, 4 barrels of hulled corn, 1 bag of meal, 600 lbs of Grees, 50 bushels meal, and 24 bushels Natchies Corn Huled.

In all, seven tons of foodstuffs constituted, more or less, the complete nutrition of the expedition. The crew of the Corps was expected to replenish its larder along the way by hunting and gathering as circumstances and conditions allowed. According to William Clark: "It requires 4 deer, or an elk and a deer, or one buffalo to supply us for 24 hours." Additionally, 193 pounds of "portable soup" were ordered as an emergency ration when stores ran out and game was scarce or unavailable. The soup was produced by boiling a broth down to a gelatinous consistency, then further drying it until it was rendered quite hard and dessicated. Not exactly a favorite with the men of the Corps, it nonetheless saved them from near starvation on a number of occasions.

Each man consumed 9 pounds of meat per day, when available, and the designated hunters of the Corps were kept busy throughout the journey. Raymond Darwin Burroughs tallied the quantity of game killed and consumed during the course of the expedition:

Deer (all species combined) 1,001	Bears, grizzly 43	Turkeys 9
	Bears, black 23	Plovers 48
Elk 375	Beaver (shot or trapped) 113	Wolves (only one eaten) 18
Bison 227	Otter 16	Indian dogs (purchased
Antelope 62	Geese and Brant 104	and consumed) 190
Bighorned sheep 35	Grouse (all species) 46	Horses 12

(From *The Natural History of the Lewis and Clark Expedition.* Michigan State University Press, 1995)

This list does not include the countless smaller or more exotic animals that were captured and eaten by the Corps, such as hawk, coyote, fox, crow, eagle, gopher, muskrat, seal, whale blubber, turtle, mussels, crab, salmon, and trout. Nor does it enumerate the unfamiliar varieties of fruits, vegetables, mushrooms, seeds, and nuts that were found to be edible. However, all are mentioned in the Journals along with detailed and sometimes lively accounts of accompanying adventures.

Deer of many species were ubiquitous in North America, and venison became a primary source of protein for the duration of the expedition. Bison figured prominently during the crossing of the Great Plains, while salmon and wapato (a starchy tuber) were the staples when the Corps roamed west of the Rockies. Their diet varied according to the changing terrain, the shifting climate, and with the passing seasons.

Of incalculable importance to the men of the Corps was the contribution of native foods by the Indian nations. The Mandan tribe of North Dakota brought them corn, squash, and beans; the Chinook living along Washington's Columbia River introduced them to wapato, a much-needed carbohydrate; and the Clatsop from the Oregon coast traded elk, wild licorice root, and berries. Shoshone tribesmen from what is now Idaho and Montana offered Lewis antelope and his first taste of salmon, and the Chopunnish (Idaho and Washington) section of the Nez Perce tribe, who ranged over Idaho, Washington, and Oregon, offered dog as well as edible roots.

During their stay at Fort Clatsop, members of the Corps developed a technique for extracting salt from seawater through evaporation by boiling. Essential not only as a flavoring, of which Lewis was fond and to which Clark was indifferent, salting was a vital method of curing and preserving meat, along with smoking and drying.

Despite the apparent bounty of the ever-changing landscape and the generosity of local tribes, many were the nights when the crew of the Corps went to sleep hungry. Many were the days when shots went awry and missed their mark or game remained hidden from sight. Relentless rain ruined drying meat, punishing heat spoiled perishable provisions, and clothing rotted right off the backs of the men. It is impossible to miss the despair in Clark's description of their privations:

SEPTEMBER 11, 1804 — he had been 12 days without any thing to eate but Grapes & one rabit, which he killed by shooting a piece of hard Stick in place of a ball . . . Thus a man had like to have Starved to death in a land of Plenty for the want of Bulits or Something to kill his meat. — CLARK

These hardships existed in sharp contrast to life along the settled Eastern Seaboard of the United States. On the frontier, living was a daily struggle for survival that revolved around the successful hunting or capture of game. Back at home, Americans flourished thanks to the bounty of fertile soils, the rewards of domestic and international commerce, the security of a common law, and the blessings of a cultivated civility.

And no one took either cultivation or civility more seriously than our third president. Jefferson was a serious horticulturist whose gracious plantation at Monticello in Virginia was a virtual state-of-the-art experimental farm. The complete plantings in his gardens, orchards, and fields contained over 250 different varieties of fruits, vegetables, and grains—with no fewer than 20 varieties of peas alone!

Following his years in Paris as ambassador to France, Jefferson's interest in food became a passion for *haute cuisine* and he returned to the United States eager to entertain with an enthusiasm that never dimmed throughout the remainder of his life. He carried his gourmet preferences with him to the White House where, we can only assume, a sophisticated new standard was set. It is most unfortunate that no menus have survived from the Jeffersonian era, although one guest at Monticello made this tantalizing report:

SEPTEMBER 1797 — They take turns giving dinner parties and teas. I was invited to one such. The meal consists of the following. The first course, two or three roast capons with a sauce of butter, cooked oysters, etc., a roast beef, some boiled mutton, some fish or ham. The second course a Pouding or tart Custards or blanc-manger and some preserves. The tablecloth is removed and fruits, almonds, grapes, chestnuts and wine are served. One drinks to the health of the President, the Vice-President, and Congress. The ladies retire; the gentlemen remain for hours in order to chat and drink toasts. Finally they join the ladies and take coffee and tea. ⇀ NIEMCEWICZ

Throughout this book appear selections from the famous Journals of Lewis and Clark, as well as from Corps members Patrick Gass, John Ordway, and Joseph White-house. Excerpts from Thomas Jefferson's copious correspondence and farm diaries offer 21st century readers insight into the agricultural and culinary history of our young republic. Readers may be less familiar with Polish author Julian Ursyn Niem-cewicz, who traveled throughout the United States from 1797–1799, returning in 1805. Niemcewicz first met Jefferson in Paris in 1787 and dined with him often in Philadelphia and at Monticello. His keen observations of people, places, events, and culture are quoted from his wonderful book *Under Their Vine and Fig Tree*.

With few exceptions, the ingredients used within these pages would have been familiar to Meriwether Lewis, William Clark, and Thomas Jefferson. All recipes are based on or inspired by recipes from historic cookbooks of the era, as well as ingredients used at the time. Exceptions are minor and have been used only when certain ingredients no longer exist or may not be readily available today. Saleratus, an early baking powder, has been substituted with modern double-acting baking powder. For obvious reasons powdered gelatin is used in place of isinglass (fish bladders) and boiled beef hooves. Finally, due to health concerns, the process of corning meat by rubbing it with salt has been replaced with immersion in a salt brine. It has also been necessary to leave out ingredients such as wapato, cul ho-mo, pash-a-co, and other indigenous foods that are gener-ally unobtainable to most readers.

It should be to no one's loss that recipes for dog and horse have been omit-ted here. One could argue the case, and doubtless someone will, for unflinching historical authenticity and including a recipe to accompany the following:

APRIL 13, 1806 ⇀ the dog now constitutes a considerable part of our subsistence and with most of the party has become a favorite food; cer-tain I am that it is a healthy strong diet, and from habit it has become by no means disagreeable to me, I prefer it to venison or Ilk, and it is very far superior to the horse in any state. ⇀ LEWIS

But to venture a foray into a cuisine fraught with the sentimental attachments we have for horse and hound would be too much, too much even when viewed with scholarly detachment. It is for this reason that the recipes in this volume have been limited to such ingredients as may be found at reputable grocers and specialty meat producers. A list of purveyors for hard-to-find ingredients is included.

The late 18th and early 19th centuries saw dramatic changes in the kitchens of America and Europe. While the Corps of Discovery labored to cook over open fires, their families back home enjoyed advances in ovens, cooking techniques, and ideas concerning food preparation. The precursor to the modern oven, the Franklin stove was developed in 1787 and was later improved upon with the Rumford oven in 1789. However, most early Americans still cooked over an open hearth.

Lewis and Clark's now famous voyage to the edge of the known world and beyond commenced on July 5, 1803, with Captain Lewis's departure from the White House. It took 2 years, 4 months, and 10 days. It is a feat that remains as freshly astonishing today as it was 200 years ago. I offer this book in tribute to an extraordinary group of visionary men who walked, paddled, starved, and shivered into American history and changed the world forever.

OCTOBER 20, 1806 ⟶ I received, my dear sir, with unspeakable joy your letter of Sep. 23 announcing the return of yourself, Capt. Clark & your party in good health to St. Louis. The unknown scenes in which you were engaged & the length of time without hearing of you had begun to be felt awfully. . . . you already know my constant affection for you & the joy with which all your friends here will receive you. ⟶ JEFFERSON

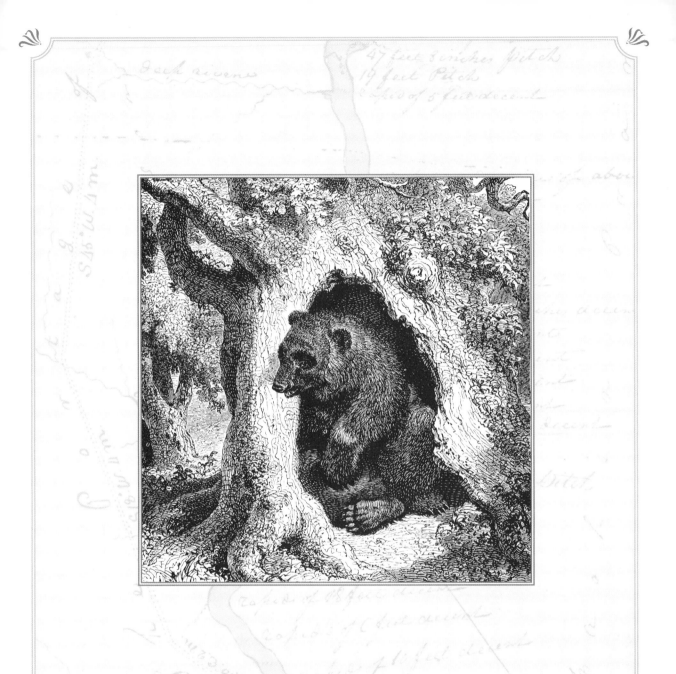

FEBRUARY 9, 1806 — in the evening Drewyer returned, had killed nothing but one beaver. He saw one black bear, which is the only one which has been seen in this neighborhood since our arrival; the Indians inform us that they are abundant but are now in their holes. — LEWIS

Gardens & Grains

Asparagus with Lemon Butter and Pine Nuts

*Described in the Journals of Lewis and Clark, pine nuts were a culinary staple
for many Native Americans. Here they are paired with asparagus,
an edible member of the lily family.*

¼ cup butter
¼ cup pine nuts
2 tablespoons freshly squeezed lemon juice
    Salt and freshly ground black pepper to taste
1 pound asparagus

In a small saucepan, melt the butter over medium-low heat. When the butter starts to sizzle, add the pine nuts and sauté until lightly golden brown and fragrant. Remove from heat and stir in the lemon juice, salt, and pepper. Set aside.

Trim the asparagus and steam just until tender. Place the asparagus in a serving dish and pour the lemon butter sauce over the top.

Serves 4 to 6

MAY 8, 1806 ⟶ . . . *near this camp I observed many pine trees which appear to have been cut down about that season which they inform us was done in order to collect the seed of the longleafed pine which in those moments of distress also furnishes an article of food, the seed of this speceis of pine is about the size and much the shape of the seed of the large sunflower; they are nutricious and not unpleasent when roasted or boiled,* ⟶ LEWIS

Green Beans with Summer Savory

*Heirloom green beans, or those whose cultivation may be traced back over fifty years
without hybridizing or crossbreeding, particularly lend themselves to this
recipe and are especially good when high quality bacon is selected for the bacon fat.
The Smithfield bacons are especially good and were used widely in the
time of Jefferson and Lewis and Clark.*

2   tablespoons bacon fat
1   pound green beans, cut in half
2   tablespoons water
2   teaspoons red wine vinegar
1   tablespoon minced fresh summer savory herb
1   teaspoon salt
½   teaspoon freshly ground black pepper

In a large skillet, heat the bacon fat over medium heat. Add the beans and sauté
for 2 minutes. Add the water, vinegar, summer savory, salt, and pepper and cover
the skillet tightly. Reduce the heat to medium-low and cook for about 10 minutes, or until tender.

Serves 6

SUMMER SAVORY

OCTOBER 6, 1810 — *When we had the pleasure of possessing
you here, you expressed a wish to have some of the Ricara
snap beans, and of the Columbian Salsafia brought from the
Western side of the continent by Gov.ᵣ Lewis. I now enclose
you some seeds of each. the Ricara bean is one of the most
excellent we have had, I have cultivated them plentifully for
the table two years.* — JEFFERSON to Benjamin S. Barton

Baked Beans

Beans were a staple in every settler's kitchen and in every explorer's saddlebag. Lightweight when dry, beans stored well, and tasted great. Hung on the swing-out cast-iron crane above the coals in the fireplace, the aroma of cooking beans lured the young farmer home after a hard day of walking behind a plow and the exhausted traveler back to camp. Have your butcher split the ham bone to expose the rich marrow, which will impart its unique flavor to the beans.

1 pound navy beans, soaked overnight
   in water to cover, then drained

1 meaty ham bone
3 cups water
2 cups diced ham
2 cups chopped tomatoes
1 onion, chopped
½ cup Tomato Catsup,
   see page 23, or ketchup·

⅓ cup packed brown sugar
2 cloves garlic, chopped
1 teaspoon salt
¾ teaspoon dry mustard
½ teaspoon freshly ground
   black pepper

Preheat oven to 350 degrees.

In a large pot, combine the ham bone with 3 cups of water. Cover the pot and simmer over low heat for 3 hours. Stir in the drained navy beans, ham, tomatoes, onion, ketchup, brown sugar, garlic, salt, dry mustard, and pepper. Cover the pot and bake for 3 to 4 hours, or until all of the liquid has been absorbed and the beans are very tender.

Serves 8

JULY 4, 1805 — our work being at an end this evening, we gave the men a drink of Sperits, it being the last of our stock, and some of them appeared a little sensible of it's effects. the fiddle was plyed and they danced very merrily untill 9 in the evening when a heavy shower or rain put an end to that part of the amusement tho' they continued their mirth with songs and festive jokes and were extreemly merry untill late at night. we had a very comfortable dinner, of bacon, beans, suit dumplings & buffaloe beaf &c. in short we had no just cause to covet the sumptuous feasts of our countrymen on this day. — LEWIS

Sweet-and-Sour Red Cabbage

Because of its hardiness, cabbage was brought to the New World by immigrants from all over Europe during the 17th and 18th centuries. Drying and preserving fruits and berries like the prunes in this recipe, were essential skills in every American kitchen.

3 tablespoons butter
1 red cabbage, cored and finely shredded
1 cup chopped pitted prunes
¾ cup red wine vinegar
½ cup red currant jelly
½ cup water
3 whole cloves
  Salt and freshly ground black pepper to taste

In a large pot, melt the butter over medium heat. Add the cabbage, prunes, vinegar, currant jelly, water, cloves, salt, and pepper and toss together. Bring the mixture to a simmer then, cover the pot, reduce heat to medium-low and cook for about 1½ hours. Stir the cabbage occasionally and add more water if the mixture gets too dry.

Serves 6

RED CABBAGE

JULY 20, 1805 — I found a black currant which I thought preferable in flavor to the yellow. This currant is really a charming fruit and I am confident would be preferred at our markets to any currant now cultivated in the U. States. — LEWIS

Endive Salad with Buttermilk Dressing

A member of the chicory family, endives were brought to North America by Dutch and Belgian immigrants. As is clear from the excerpt below, the availability of endives during the winter months provided much-needed greens for the Jeffersonian table.

½ cup buttermilk
1 tablespoon olive oil
1 tablespoon cider vinegar
¼ teaspoon salt
¼ teaspoon freshly ground black pepper
3 endives, sliced

In a bowl, whisk together the buttermilk, olive oil, vinegar, salt, and pepper. Add the endives and toss to coat with the dressing.

Serves 4

MARCH 21, 1802 — *Would it be within the scope of mr Bailey's plan of gardening for the common market, to make a provision of endive for the ensuing winter, so as to be able to furnish Th: J. with a sallad of endive every day through the winter until spring sallading should commence,* — JEFFERSON to Robert Bailey

PLATE I

MARMOTS AND PRAIRIE DOG

SEPTEMBER 7, 1804 — discovered a Village of Small animals that burrow in the grown (those animals are Called by the french Petite Chien) . . . the Village of those animals Cov⁴. about 4 acres of Ground on a gradual decent of a hill and Contains great numbers of holes on the top of which those little animals Set erect make a Whistleing noise and whin allarmed Step into their hole. Those Animals are about the Size of a Small Squ[ir]rel Shorter (or longer) & thicker, the head much resembling a Squirel in every respect, except the ears which is Shorter, . . . the toe nails long, they have fine fur & the longer hairs is gray, — CLARK

Hominy with Tomatoes au Gratin

*Produced by soaking corn in lye until the hulls dissolve and the kernels puff,
hominy was another Native American food eagerly adopted by the settlers
and frontiersmen. Still a staple in the South, this recipe combines
hominy with tomatoes, yet another New World fruit.
This is an excellent side dish for pork, veal, and baked fowl.*

3 cups cooked white hominy, drained
2 cups chopped tomatoes
2 tablespoons fine dry bread crumbs
1 teaspoon minced fresh sage
1 teaspoon salt
½ teaspoon freshly ground black pepper
1 cup shredded Cheddar cheese

Preheat oven to 350 degrees. Lightly oil a 9 by 9-inch baking dish.

Spread the hominy in the prepared baking dish. Spread the tomatoes evenly
over the hominy. Sprinkle the bread crumbs, sage, salt, and pepper over the
tomatoes. Top with the cheese and bake for 30 minutes.

Serves 6

SAGE

AUGUST 17, 1805 — *we also distributed a good quantity
paint mockerson awles knives beads looking-glasses &c among
the other Indians and gave them a plentifull meal of lyed
(hull taken off by being boiled in lye) corn which
was the first they had ever eaten in their lives. They were
much pleased with it.* — LEWIS

Black-Eyed Peas with Salt Pork

Salt pork is essentially bacon that has not been smoked. Salting is a traditional method of preserving the deliciously fatty pork belly. It lends creaminess to dishes where it is used and is a traditional accompaniment to a pot of black-eyed peas. Cooking with vegetable oil or butter are essentially 20th century conventions. The 18th and 19th century cooks always had a crock of salt pork or bacon on the kitchen table.

1   pound dried black-eyed peas
2   quarts water
1   tablespoon olive oil
8   ounces (about 1 cup) diced salt pork
1   onion, chopped
1   carrot, sliced
2   cloves garlic, minced
4   cups chicken stock
3   Roma tomatoes, chopped
    Salt and freshly ground black pepper to taste
½   cup chopped scallions

In a large pot or Dutch oven stir together the black-eyed peas and water. Bring to a boil over high heat and let boil for 2 minutes. Remove the pot from the heat, cover the pot, and let stand for 1 hour. Drain the peas through a colander.

Return the pot to medium heat and add the oil and salt pork. Sauté until the pork is lightly browned. Add the onion, carrot, and garlic and sauté until tender. Stir in the reserved peas, stock, tomatoes, salt, and pepper. Bring the mixture to a boil over medium heat, then reduce the heat to medium-low, cover the pot, and simmer for 1 hour. Uncover the pot and simmer an additional 10 to 15 minutes, or until the mixture has slightly thickened, stirring often to prevent scorching. Serve in bowls and sprinkle with chopped scallions.

Serves 6 to 8

JULY 13, 1774 ～ *black eyed peas come to table* ～ JEFFERSON

Minted Peas

*A hardy Mediterranean native, mint was already a garden staple during the time of
Lewis and Clark. It was used as a tea and as a flavoring and fragrant scent herb.
Peas were indispensable as they were easily dried and stored for winter consumption.*

2 tablespoons water
1 tablespoon butter
1 tablespoon minced fresh mint
¼ teaspoon salt
¼ teaspoon sugar
2 cups fresh shelled peas

In a saucepan, combine the water, butter, mint, salt, and sugar. Bring the mixture to a simmer over medium heat. Stir in the peas and cover the saucepan. Reduce the heat to medium-low and continue to simmer until the peas are cooked. Remove the lid from the saucepan and cook until the liquid has evaporated and the peas are glazed with the butter mixture.

Serves 6

PEAS

JUNE 25, 1805 — *great quantities of mint also are here it
resemble[s] the pepper mint very much in taste
and appearance.* — LEWIS

Parsnip Fritters

Parsnips are harvested in the late fall and were one of the group of winter vegetables essential to the colonists. These spicy roots with their velvety texture when cooked, were a versatile American staple. These parsnip fritters are an elegant accompaniment to a dish of beef, buffalo, or other wild game.

1½ pounds parsnips, peeled, sliced and steamed until tender
 2 tablespoons butter
 1 tablespoon minced shallots
 1 egg, beaten
 1 teaspoon salt
 ¼ teaspoon pepper
 2 tablespoons fine dry bread crumbs
    Oil for frying

Place the steamed parsnips in a bowl and mash until smooth. Stir in the butter, shallots, egg, salt, and pepper and combine until smooth. Stir in the bread crumbs until thoroughly blended. In a large skillet, add oil to a depth of 1 inch. Heat the oil over medium-high heat. When the oil is hot, carefully drop the parsnip mixture by the tablespoonful into the oil without crowding. Cook the parsnip fritters until golden brown on both sides. Drain on paper towels and keep warm in a 200-degree oven. Serve hot.

Serves 6 to 8

MAY 2, 1806 — *the flower and fructification resembles that of the parsnip this plant is very common in the rich lands on the Ohio and it's branches the Mississippi &c. I tasted of this plant and found it agreeable and eat heartily of it without feeling any inconvenience.* — LEWIS

Potato Croquettes

The potato is truly one of the great gifts from the New World. Originally from South and Central America, the first wild varieties were cultivated by ancient Americans. Spanish explorers brought the potato to Europe in the 15th century where it was heavily cultivated and hybridized and later brought back to North America by the early settlers.

1   pound potatoes, peeled and cut into 2-inch cubes
¼   cup freshly grated Parmesan cheese
1   egg, lightly beaten
2   tablespoons minced onion
1   tablespoon minced fresh parsley
1   clove garlic, minced
   Salt and freshly ground black pepper to taste
2   cups fresh bread crumbs, divided
   Olive oil for frying

In a large pot, combine the potatoes and enough salted water to cover. Bring to a boil over medium-high heat, and cook until the potatoes are very tender. Drain the potatoes and mash until smooth. Set aside to cool.

In a large bowl, whisk together the Parmesan, egg, onion, parsley, garlic, salt, and pepper. Add the mashed potatoes and stir until just combined. Add 1 cup of the bread crumbs and stir until just blended. Form the mixture into walnut-sized balls and roll in the remaining bread crumbs. In a large skillet, heat ⅛-inch of olive oil over medium-high heat. Add the croquettes, reduce heat to medium, and fry until golden brown on all sides. Drain on paper towels and serve immediately.

Serves 4 to 6

NOVEMBER 4, 1805 — *The roots are of a superior quality to any I had before seen; they are called whapto, resemble a potatoe when cooked, and are about as big as a hen egg.* — GASS

Potatoes au Gratin

*During a July 4th celebration in 1802, a delegation from Pennsylvania sent
President Jefferson a 1200-pound "mammoth cheese" with the inscription
"the greatest cheese in America for the greatest man in America."
Jefferson never accepted gifts, so he paid for it out of his personal account,
and in his ledger book he noted: "to the bearer of the cheese $200."*

  4 pounds potatoes

Cheese Sauce:
  ¼ cup butter
  3 tablespoons all-purpose flour
  ¼ cup finely minced onion
  1 teaspoon salt
  ½ teaspoon freshly ground black pepper
  3 cups milk
  3 cups lightly packed, grated, sharp Cheddar cheese
     Paprika

Preheat oven to 350 degrees. Lightly oil a 9 by 13-inch baking dish.

In a large pot, cover the potatoes with water and bring to a boil. Cook the potatoes, in their jackets, over medium heat until barely tender when pierced with a fork. Drain the potatoes and let cool slightly. Peel the potatoes and discard the skin. Thickly slice the potatoes and set aside.

For the cheese sauce: In a large saucepan, melt the butter over medium heat. Whisk in the flour and continue stirring until the mixture is bubbly, but do not let it brown. Stir in the onion, salt, and pepper. Add the milk slowly in a thin stream, whisking constantly until the mixture thickens. Remove the saucepan from the heat and briskly stir in the cheese until smooth.

Layer the potato slices and the cheese sauce alternately in the prepared baking dish, starting with a layer of potatoes, then cheese sauce, then potatoes, and ending with the cheese sauce. Sprinkle with the paprika. Bake for about 45 minutes, or until the potatoes are very tender and the top is golden brown.

Serves 8 to 10

AUGUST 2, 1797 — *we saw women engaged in making cheese. Cheese, milk, butter, potatoes and boiled or baked corn is the principal food of the farmer.* — NIEMCEWICZ

12

PLATE II

WOLVERINE, BADGER, AND OTTERS

FEBRUARY 23, 1806 — it is the richest and I think the most delightfull fur in the world at least I cannot form an idea of any more so. it is deep thick silky in the extream and strong. the inner part of the fur when open is lighter than the surface in its natural position. there are some fine black shining hairs intermixed with the fur which are reather longer and add much to its beauty. the nose, about the eyes, ears and forehead in some of those otter is of a light colour, sometimes a light brown . . . the Indians call the infant otter spuck, and the full grown or such as had obtained a coat of good fur, E-luck'ko. — CLARK

Salsify with Shallots and Chives

Salsify is a winter root vegetable native to North America that has a faintly oyster-like flavor and was in fact known as the oyster plant and the vegetable oyster as early as 1690. It is particularly good with slow-braised roasts of beef or buffalo. Salsify quickly discolors, so immediately place it in cold water with vinegar as soon as it is pared.

2   quarts water
¼   cup cider vinegar
1½ pounds salsify, peeled and cut into 1-inch pieces
3   tablespoons butter
2   tablespoons minced shallots
    Salt and freshly ground black pepper to taste
2   tablespoons minced fresh chives

In a pot, combine the water, cider vinegar, and salsify. Bring to a boil over high heat, then reduce the heat to medium, and simmer for about 20 minutes, or until tender.

In a skillet, melt the butter over medium heat. Add the shallots and sauté until fragrant. Drain the salsify and add it to the skillet. Sauté until lightly browned. Season with salt and pepper. Sprinkle with the chives and serve.

Serves 4

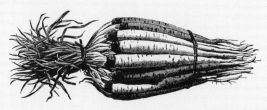

SALSIFY

DECEMBER 14, 1812 ⟶ *I do not remember to have seen Salsafia in your garden, & yet it is one of the best roots for the winter. some call it oyster plant because fried in butter it can scarcely be distinguished from a fried oyster. I send you some seed. it is to be sowed and managed as carrots & to be taken up at the same time & put away for winter use.*
⟶ JEFFERSON to Charles Clay

Wine-Glazed Sunchokes

Also known as Jerusalem artichokes, these potato-like tubers supported the men of the Corps of Discovery during times when there was little else to eat. Nutty in flavor with a creamy potato-like texture when cooked, sunchokes are a delicious and nutritious side dish, and heartily deserve to be part of today's cuisine.

2 tablespoons olive oil
2 tablespoons minced shallots
1 clove garlic, minced
1 pound sunchokes, scrubbed and thinly sliced
½ cup dry white wine
¼ teaspoon dried thyme
   Salt and freshly ground black pepper to taste

In a skillet, heat the olive oil over medium heat. Add the shallots and sauté until tender. Add the garlic and sauté until fragrant. Add the sunchokes and sauté for 2 minutes. Add the wine and the thyme, cover the skillet and cook for 10 minutes. Remove the lid and sauté until the liquid has evaporated. Season with salt and pepper and serve immediately.

Serves 6

JERUSALEM ARTICHOKES

APRIL 9, 1805 — *when we halted for dinner the [Sacagawea] busied herself in serching for the wild artichokes which the mice collect and deposit in large hoards. this operation she performed by penetrating the earth with a sharp stick about some small collections of driftwood. her labour soon proved successful, and she procured a good quantity of these roots.* — LEWIS

Homemade Noodles

*Even if you have a pasta maker to roll out the sheets of dough, try slicing
the noodles by hand. The varying width of hand-cut pasta makes a big difference
in the flavor and texture. You can either boil the noodles immediately,
or hang them over a rack or line to dry. The flavor of freshly made noodles is
vastly superior to the dried store-bought varieties.*

2 cups all-purpose flour
3 eggs, lightly beaten

Sift the flour into a large bowl and make a well in the center. Pour the eggs into
the well. Stir with a fork until the dough becomes soft but not sticky. Turn the
dough out on a lightly floured work surface and knead until smooth and satiny,
about 7 minutes. Cover the dough and let rest for about 1 hour.

Divide the dough into 4 portions. On a lightly floured surface, roll out each portion of the dough to approximately ⅛-inch thickness. Cut noodles to desired
thickness. Bring a large pot of salted water to a boil. Cook the pasta until al dente,
then drain.

Serves 6

NOVEMBER 12, 1790 — *I inclose you some wheat which
the President assures me from many years experience
to be the best kind he has ever seen. he spread it through the
Eastern shore of Maryland several years ago, and it has
ever been considered as the best of the white wheat of that
state so much celebrated.* — JEFFERSON to Thomas Mann Randolph

Noodles with Pine Nuts, Parmesan, and Sweet Oil

During his travels in Italy, Jefferson enjoyed what we know as pasta al pesto.
All these ingredients were readily obtainable in Jefferson's garden.
Olive oil was known as sweet oil in 18th century America.
The pine nuts were a staple food of many Native American tribes.
For an interesting variation, use the Homemade Noodles on page 15.

¾ cup pine nuts
1 cup packed fresh basil leaves
½ cup freshly grated Parmesan cheese
1 teaspoon minced garlic
   Salt and freshly ground black pepper to taste
½ cup olive oil
1 pound spaghetti, cooked in boiling salted water
   until al dente, then drained

Preheat oven to 350 degrees.

Spread the pine nuts on a rimmed baking sheet. Toast them in the oven for about 5 minutes, stirring occasionally, so that the nuts toast evenly. Let the pine nuts cool completely.

In the bowl of a food processor or blender, combine the pine nuts, basil, Parmesan, garlic, salt, and pepper. Pulse, scraping down the sides often, until the mixture is ground to a coarse paste. With the motor running, add the olive oil in a thin stream. The mixture will be creamy. Toss the hot noodles with the sauce in a large bowl and serve immediately.

Serves 6

JULY 30, 1787 — *the olive is a tree the least known in America, and yet the most worthy of being known. Of all the gifts of heaven to man, it is next to the most precious, if it be not the most precious. Perhaps it may claim a preference even to bread, because there is such an infinitude of vegetables, which it renders a proper and comfortable nourishment.* — JEFFERSON to William Drayton

Macaroni and Cheese

*In the 18th century, macaroni was formed by passing pasta dough through
bronze dies which gave the pasta a more textured surface.
Sauces stuck much better to this traditional pasta, unlike today's smooth
Teflon die-formed pasta. But the the old-fashioned type is still available
in specialty grocery stores and it definitely pays to ask for it.*

3	tablespoons butter
2	tablespoons all-purpose flour
1	teaspoon salt
½	teaspoon dry mustard
¼	teaspoon cayenne
¼	teaspoon freshly ground black pepper
2	cups milk
½	cup heavy cream
2	cups shredded Cheddar cheese
12	ounces macaroni, cooked in boiling salted water, then drained

Preheat oven to 350 degrees. Lightly oil a 9 by 13-inch baking dish.

In a large saucepan, melt the butter over medium heat. Whisk in the flour, salt,
mustard, cayenne, and black pepper and cook, stirring constantly until bubbly.
Slowly pour in the milk and cream in a thin stream, whisking constantly. Reduce
the heat to a simmer, and continue to whisk, until the mixture has thickened.
Remove the saucepan from the heat and stir in the cheese until melted. Stir in
the macaroni, then transfer to the prepared baking dish. Bake for about 20 minutes, or until hot and bubbly.

Serves 6 to 8

FEBRUARY 6, 1802 — *Dined at the President's — Rice soup,
round of beef, turkey, mutton, ham, loin of veal, cutlets of
mutton or veal, fried eggs, fried beef, a pie called macaroni, which
appeared to be a rich crust filled with scallion of onions or
shallots, which I took it to be, tasted very strong, and not very
agreeable. Mr. Lewis told me there was none in it, it was an
Italian dish, and what appeared like onions were made of flour
and butter, with a particularly strong liquor mixed with them.*
— SENATOR MANASSEH CUTLER of Massachusetts

Rice Pilaf

Of immense interest to the American farmers by the 18th century, rice was an important export item for the United States. While Ambassador to France, under pain of death if caught, Jefferson smuggled a pocketful of special rice out of Italy to experiment with its cultivation at Monticello. Serve this savory side dish with rabbit, goose, or pork tenderloin.

2 tablespoons butter
1 cup long grain rice
½ cup slivered almonds
1½ cups chicken stock
1 teaspoon salt
⅛ teaspoon ground mace

In a saucepan, melt the butter over medium heat. Add the rice and almonds and sauté until lightly golden. Stir in the stock, salt, and mace and bring to a simmer. Reduce the heat to low, cover the saucepan, and cook for about 20 minutes, or until all of the liquid is absorbed.

Serves 4

OCTOBER 4, 1790 — *The seeds [of mountain rice] I have at present came from the Island of Timor in the East Indies, brought by the unfortunate Capt. Bligh.* — SAMUEL VAUGHN, JR. to Jefferson

PLATE III

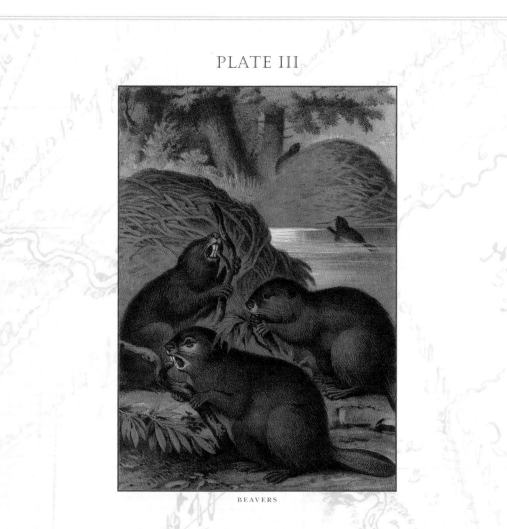

BEAVERS

AUGUST 2, 1805 — We saw some very large beaver dams today in the bottoms of the river several of which wer five feet high and overflowed several acres of land, these dams are formed of willow brush mud and gravel and are so closely interwoven that they resist the water perfectly. the base of this work is thick and rises nearly perpendicularly on the lower side while the upper side or that within the dam is gently sloped. The brush appear to be laid in no regular order yet acquires a strength by the irregularity with which they are placed by the beaver that it would puzzle the engenuity of man to give them. — LEWIS

III

Wild Rice with Chestnuts

*The first domesticated chestnuts were known to have been brought from Europe to
the American colonies as early as the 17th century. Wild rice, which is actually
a type of wild grass, was another gift from the Native Americans to the early
settlers of Minnesota and Wisconsin.*

3½ cups chicken stock
1½ cups wild rice
1 teaspoon salt
1 bay leaf
½ teaspoon dried thyme
20 whole chestnuts

2 tablespoons butter
1 cup chopped onion
1 carrot, chopped
1 stalk celery, chopped
2 cloves garlic, minced

Preheat oven to 350 degrees.

In a large saucepan, combine the chicken stock, rice, salt, bay leaf, and thyme.
Bring to a boil, then reduce the heat to medium-low, cover the saucepan, and
simmer for 30 minutes.

With a sharp paring knife, score each chestnut with an X on the flat side of the
chestnut. Place the chestnuts in a saucepan and cover them with water. Bring to
a boil, then reduce the heat to medium-low and simmer for 25 minutes. Drain
the chestnuts and remove the shell and bitter membrane. Spread the chestnuts
out on a baking sheet and toast them for about 7 minutes in the oven. Coarsely
chop the chestnuts and set aside.

In a skillet, melt the butter over medium heat. Add the onion and sauté until
tender. Add the carrot and celery and sauté until tender. Add the garlic and
sauté until fragrant. After the wild rice has simmered for 30 minutes, stir in the
onion mixture and reserved chestnuts. Cover the saucepan and simmer an additional 20 minutes, or until all of the liquid has been absorbed.

Serves 6

MARCH 1,1798 — *I had dinner at Mr. Mackluer's with
Dr Scandella, Mr. Volney and Vice-President Jefferson. The
instructive and interesting conversation of these persons made
time fly by quickly. The Dr. showed us a bag of Wild Rice and
wild oats, Zizania Aquatica, grains which grow wild in marshy
places in all of America up to Hudson Bay.* — NIEMCEWICZ

19

Curried Wild Rice and Smoked Chicken Salad

Few American foods are as evocative of the great outdoors as wild rice. Long a staple of the Chippewa and Sioux Indians in the regions of Wisconsin and Minnesota, wild rice was slower to be adopted by the Europeans than other native grains such as corn. This recipe combines a uniquely American ingredient with an exotic spice blend treasured by cooks of the Jeffersonian era.

1½ pounds boneless skinless
    chicken thighs
Alder chips for smoking

1¼ cups wild rice
3¼ cups water
1 teaspoon salt

½ cup dried cranberries
½ cup chopped scallions

Dressing:
⅔ cup olive oil
½ cup sour cream
2 tablespoons freshly squeezed lemon juice
2 tablespoons white wine vinegar
2 cloves garlic, minced
2 teaspoons curry powder
1 teaspoon salt
½ teaspoon freshly ground black pepper
½ teaspoon sugar

Smoke the chicken for 1 hour with the wood chips. Remove the chicken from the smoker and broil or grill the chicken to finish cooking. Cut the chicken into ½-inch dice and set aside.

In a large saucepan, stir together the wild rice, water, and salt. Bring to a boil over high heat, then reduce the heat to low, and cover saucepan. Simmer the wild rice for about 50 minutes, or until the wild rice has absorbed all of the water.

In a large bowl, whisk together the olive oil, sour cream, lemon juice, vinegar, garlic, curry powder, salt, pepper, and sugar. Stir in the hot wild rice until it is completely coated. Stir in the reserved smoked chicken, dried cranberries, and scallions. Chill before serving.

Serves 6

Curry powder is used as a fine flavoured seasoning for fish, fowls, steaks, chops, veal cutlets, hashes, minces, alamodes, turtle soup, and in all rich dishes, gravies, sauce, &c. &c.
— *The Virginia Housewife* by MRS. MARY RANDOLPH, 1828

Spiced Watermelon Rind

Another gift to the settlers from the Indians, watermelons were quickly adapted as sweet pickles to enjoy all year round. If you have a selection of small cookie cutters, use them to create fanciful shapes after peeling the tough green outer skin off the watermelon rind. A small block of wood can then be used to press the cutter through the rind. These pickles are firm and have a wonderful sweet/sour tangy flavor.

1 watermelon
2 quarts water
⅓ cup noniodized salt
4 cups sugar
2 cups distilled white vinegar
1 lemon, sliced
3 cinnamon sticks
1 tablespoon whole allspice berries
1 tablespoon whole cloves

Cut the rind of the watermelon into manageable pieces. Cut off all of the outer green skin and inner pink flesh. Cut the rind into 1-inch square pieces. You should have about 10 cups of prepared rind. In a large bowl, stir together the water and salt. Add the rind, cover the bowl, and let stand overnight. Drain and rinse the rind. In a large pot, combine the drained rind with enough fresh water to cover. Simmer over medium heat for about 15 minutes, or until tender.

In a large pot, combine the sugar and vinegar. Tie the lemon slices, cinnamon sticks, allspice, and cloves in a piece of cheesecloth and add to the pot. Add the watermelon rind and bring to a simmer over medium heat. Simmer for about 35 to 40 minutes, or until the rind is transparent. With a slotted spoon, divide the rind between 3 sterilized pint jars. Fill the jars with the syrup, leaving a ½-inch headspace. Wipe the rims of the jars and adjust the lids. Process the jars in a boiling water bath for 10 minutes.

Makes 3 pints

AUGUST 2, 1804 — *... among those Indians 6 were Chiefs (not the principal Chiefs) Capt. Lewis and myself met those Indians & informed them we were glad to see them, and would speak to them tomorrow, Sent them some roasted meat, Pork flour & meal, in return they sent us Water millions* — CLARK

Sweet Hot Mustard

Cultivated since Biblical times, mustard flourished in American gardens as well.
Incredible with Smithfield ham, this sweet, hot mustard is great with roast pork
and sauerkraut, sausage, and as a spread on sandwiches.

½ cup sugar
2 eggs
⅔ cup dry mustard
½ cup malt vinegar

In the top of a double-boiler, whisk together the sugar and eggs until smooth.
Whisk in the mustard until smooth. Add the vinegar in a thin stream, whisking
until all is incorporated. Place the double-boiler over simmering water and cook,
whisking constantly, until the mixture has thickened. Serve the mustard at room
temperature. Store covered in the refrigerator.

Makes about 1 cup

MARCH 26, 1777 — *sowed radishes, lettuce, endive,*
& red mustard. — JEFFERSON

Tomato Catsup

With a homemade sauce one may vary ingredients and proportions to suit individual tastes. Although this recipe makes a most wonderful catsup, feel free to vary the ingredients to come up with your own "heirloom" recipe.

10	cups chopped tomatoes
2	cups chopped onions
1½	cups packed brown sugar
1½	cups distilled white vinegar
¼	cup pickling spice
1½	teaspoons salt
½	teaspoon paprika

In a large pot, combine all the ingredients. Bring to a boil, reduce heat to medium-low, and simmer partially covered for 1 hour, stirring occasionally. Remove the lid and continue to simmer until mixture is very thick, stirring often to prevent scorching. When the mixture is thick, pour through a fine sieve into a bowl, pressing on the solids. Discard the remaining solids. The catsup will keep covered, in the refrigerator for about 1 month.

Makes about 3 cups

TOMATOES

1782 — *The gardens yield musk melons, water melons, tomatas, okra, pomegranates, figs, and the esculent plants of Europe.* — JEFFERSON

Hot Pepper Sauce

Hot pepper sauce was just coming into fashion during Jefferson's era.
Chile peppers were yet another contribution to the world's cuisine from America.
Ubiquitous now all over the world, from Europe to Asia, there is hardly a cuisine
that hasn't adopted the fiery chile pepper.

2 pounds fresh hot chiles
4 cups cider vinegar
4 teaspoons noniodized salt

Take care when working with the chiles because the volatile oils can burn eyes if touched.

Remove the stems from the chiles. Place the chiles in the bowl of a food processor, in batches, and process until coarsely chopped. In a pot, combine the chiles, cider vinegar, and salt. Bring the mixture to a boil, then reduce heat to medium-low and simmer for 5 minutes. Transfer the mixture to an earthenware crock and allow to cool. Cover the crock and let stand in a cool area for 1 month. Strain the mixture through cheesecloth and discard the solids. Pour the sauce into bottles and cap tightly. Store in a cool, dark place.

Makes about 4 cups

JUNE 13, 1813 — I hope that the small package of Capsicum, which I sent you, a few weeks ago has arrived in safety. You may even a month hence be very certain of obtaining Plants which, with a little care, can be preserved through the Winter & which will yeild fruit before the last of May. I now send you as much as you will be able to use until that time. The Spaniards generally use it in fine Powder & seldom eat anything without it. The Americans who have learned to use it make a Pickle of the green Pods with Salt & Vinegar which they use with Lettuce, Rice, Fish, Beefstake, and almost every other dish. a single Tablespoonful will communicate to as much Vinegar as I can use in six months, as strong a taste of Capsicum as I find agreeable & I find this taste growing so fast that it will soon become as essential to my health as salt itself. — SAMUEL BROWN to Jefferson

JUNE 15, 1813 — I have just received some Capsicum of the province of Techas, where it is indigenous as far Eastwardly as the Sabine river. it's roots are perennial there, and it is believed it will stand our frosts with a little covering. it grows in great abundance there and the inhabitants are in the habit of using it as a seasoning for everything as freely as salt, and ascribe much of their health to it.

— JEFFERSON to Bernard McMahon

PEPPERS

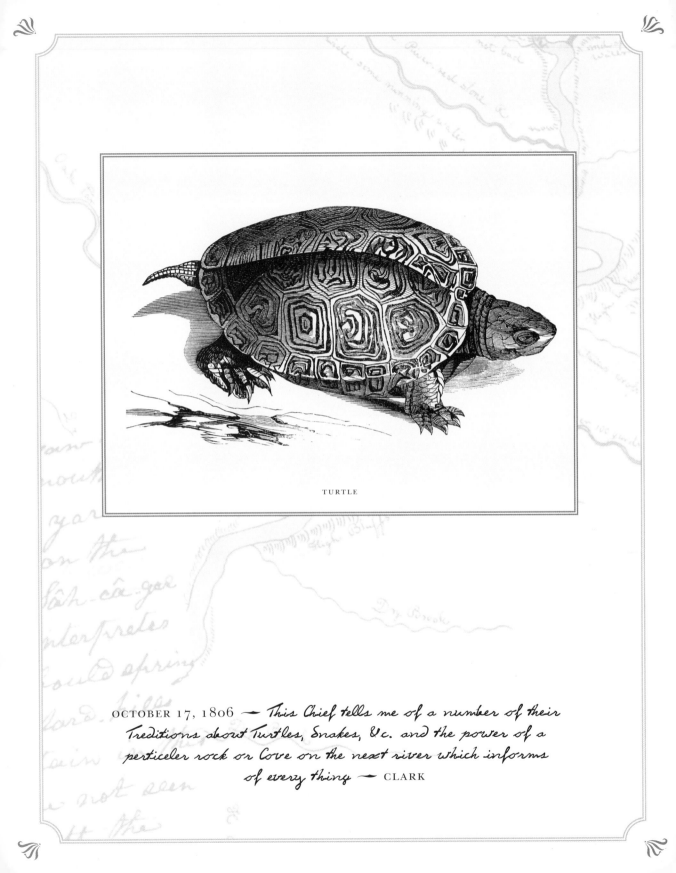

TURTLE

OCTOBER 17, 1806 — *This Chief tells me of a number of their Treditions about Turtles, Snakes, &c. and the power of a perticeler rock or Cove on the next river which informs of every thing* — CLARK

Soups

Morel Mushroom Soup en Croûte

This pastry crust is quite unusual, incorporating cream cheese. It is incredibly flaky and tasty and would work well for both sweet as well as savory fillings. If you do not have access to dried morels, other dried mushrooms such as chanterelles, porcini, or shiitake will give an excellent flavor to this soup.

Cream Cheese Pastry:
- ½ cup all-purpose flour
- ¼ cup cold butter, cut into small pieces
- 2 ounces cold cream cheese, cut into small pieces
- ¼ teaspoon salt

Morel Mushroom Soup:
- 1 cup dried morel mushrooms
- 1 cup water
- 3 tablespoons butter
- 2 scallions, pale green part only, chopped
- 1 tablespoon minced shallots
- 1 clove garlic, minced
- 1 pound button mushrooms, thinly sliced
- ½ teaspoon dried thyme
- ½ cup dry sherry
- 2 cups half-and-half
- 1½ teaspoons salt
- ½ teaspoon freshly ground black pepper

For the cream cheese pastry: In the bowl of a food processor, combine the flour, butter, cream cheese, and salt. Pulse until the dough comes together. Form the dough into a ball, wrap it in plastic wrap, and flatten into a disc. Chill for 1 hour before rolling out.

In a small saucepan, combine the morels and the water. Bring to a simmer over medium heat, then remove from heat, cover the saucepan, and let stand for 30 minutes. With a slotted spoon, transfer the morels to a cutting board and finely chop them. Set the morels aside. Strain the morel soaking liquid through a fine sieve lined with a double layer of moistened cheesecloth. Set aside the strained liquid.

In a large saucepan, melt the butter over medium heat. Add the scallions, shallots, and garlic and sauté just until fragrant. Add the button mushrooms and thyme and sauté until tender. Add the reserved morels and sauté until most of the liquid has evaporated. Stir in the sherry and simmer until the liquid has reduced by half. Stir in the reserved morel liquid and simmer until the liquid has reduced by half. Stir in the half-and-half and simmer for 10 minutes.

Preheat oven to 350 degrees.

Turn the dough out onto a lightly floured surface and roll out to ¼-inch thick. Cut out circles to fit ovenproof bowls with a ½-inch overhang. Divide the soup into the 4 bowls, about 1 cup of soup in each bowl. Adjust the pastry circles over the tops of the bowls. Place the bowls on a baking sheet and set in the oven. Bake for 20 minutes, or until the pastry crusts are lightly browned. Serve immediately.

Serves 4

MUSHROOMS

JUNE 19, 1806 — *Cruzatte brought me several large morells which I roasted and eat without salt pepper or grease in this way I had for the first time the true taist of the morell which is truly an insippid taistless food.* — LEWIS

Shrimp Bisque

*The secret to a great bisque, be it crab, lobster, or shrimp, is to release the flavor
hidden in the shells through sautéing, simmering, and straining.
The liquid left behind contains an intensity of flavor, which can not be achieved
any other way. There are no modern short cuts, so relax and make it the
old-fashioned way. This is a beautiful first course soup for holiday entertaining*

1 pound fresh medium shrimp in their shells
3 tablespoons butter
¾ cup chopped onion
¼ cup brandy
6 cups clam juice
1 carrot, chopped
1 stalk celery, chopped
¼ cup chopped fresh parsley
1 clove garlic, chopped
½ teaspoon freshly ground black pepper
½ teaspoon dried tarragon
¼ teaspoon dried thyme
1 cup heavy cream

Peel the shrimp, reserving the shells, and set aside the meat. In a pot, melt the
butter over medium heat. Add the shrimp shells and sauté until they turn pink.
Add the onion, and sauté until tender. Stir in the brandy and bring to a simmer.
Stir in the clam juice, carrot, celery, parsley, garlic, pepper, tarragon, and thyme
and bring to a boil. Reduce the heat to medium-low, cover the pot, and simmer
for 30 minutes. Remove the lid from the pot and simmer an additional 30 minutes. Strain the broth through a sieve and discard the solids. Return the broth to
the pot and bring to a simmer over medium heat. Add the reserved shrimp and
simmer until they turn pink. Stir in the cream and heat through.

Serves 6 to 8

AUGUST 15, 1804 — *I cought a Srimp prosisely of Shape Size
& flavour on those about N. Orleans & the lower part
of the Mississippi...* — CLARK

PLATE IV

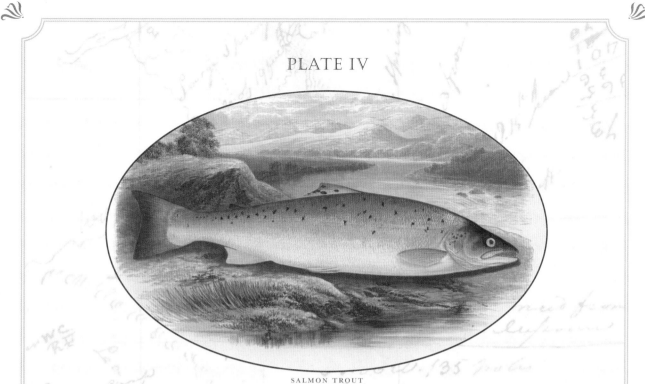

SALMON TROUT

MARCH 16, 1806 — The white Salmon Trout which we had previously seen only at the great falls of the Columbia has now made it's appearance in the creeks near this place. one of them was brought us today by an Indian who had just taken it with his gig. this is a likness of it, it was 2 feet 8 Inches long, and weighed 10 lbs. the eye is moderately large, the puple black and iris of a silvery white with a small addmixture of yellow, and is a little terbid near it's border with a yellowish brown. the position of the fins may be seen from the drawing, they are small in proportion to the fish, the fins are boney but not pointed except the tail and back fins which are a little so. the prime back fin and ventral ones, contain each ten rays; those of the gills thirteen, that of the tail twelve, and the small fins placed near the tail above has no bony rays, but is a tough flexable substance covered with smooth skin. it is thicker in proportion to it's width than the salmon. . . . neither this fish nor the salmon are caught with the hook, nor do I know on what they feed. — LEWIS

Cream of Sorrel Soup

Sorrel is an herb which was believed to "purify the blood" after a long winter without fresh greens. Because it thrives in cool weather and can be harvested as early as January in some places, sorrel was a harbinger of the goodness of the garden to come. This slightly tart and creamy soup was a favorite of Thomas Jefferson.

¼ cup butter
1 onion, chopped
12 ounces fresh sorrel, chopped
3 cups chicken stock
1 cup heavy cream
1 egg yolk
Salt and freshly ground black pepper to taste

In a large saucepan, melt the butter over medium heat. Add the onion and sauté until translucent but not browned. Add the sorrel and sauté until wilted. Stir in the chicken stock and bring to a simmer. Reduce heat to medium-low, cover the saucepan, and simmer for 30 minutes. Purée the soup in batches in a blender, then strain through a sieve, pressing on the solids. Return the soup to the saucepan and discard the solids. In a small bowl, whisk together the cream and egg yolk until smooth. Whisk the cream mixture into the soup and heat through but do not let the soup boil or it will curdle. Season with salt and pepper. This soup can be served hot or chilled.

Serves 4 to 6

SORREL

JUNE 5, 1804 ➵ . . . *my Servent York Swam to the Sand bar to geather Greens for our Dinner, and returned with a Sufficent quantity wild Creases [Cresses] or Tung [Tongue] grass . . .* ➵ CLARK

Cream of Tomato Soup

*Introduced to Europe from America in the 1600s, tomatoes were at first considered
poisonous, but quickly found their first supporters in Spain where the Aztec name*
tomatl *was changed to* tomate. *Tomatoes were a cherished vegetable in the gardens
at Monticello and were regularly enjoyed at the tables of Thomas Jefferson.*

3 tablespoons butter
1 medium onion, finely chopped
3 pounds ripe tomatoes, peeled, seeded, and chopped
2 tablespoons packed brown sugar
1 tablespoon minced fresh basil
1 bay leaf
1 teaspoon salt
½ teaspoon freshly ground black pepper
2 whole cloves
1½ cups half-and-half
    Snipped fresh chives, for garnish

In a large saucepot, melt the butter over medium heat. Add the onion and sauté
until very tender. Add the tomatoes, brown sugar, basil, bay leaf, salt, black pepper, and cloves and stir well. Reduce the heat to low, cover, and simmer until
tomatoes are cooked through, about 30 minutes. Remove the bay leaf and cloves
and discard. Purée the soup in batches in a blender. Return the puréed soup to
the pot and stir in the half-and-half. Heat the soup through over low heat, being
careful not to let it boil. Serve topped with the chives.

Serves 6

JANUARY 22, 1809 — *J. Mason presents his respects
to the President, and with very great pleasure sends him
the garden seeds asked in his note of the other day, in addition
to which he begs his acceptance of a few of the Buda-Kale—
an excellent kind of Cantaleup—Spanish tomato
(very much larger than the common kinds)—and Estragon,
from the plant the President was so good as to send
J. M a year or two ago,* — GENERAL JOHN MASON to Jefferson

Turtle Soup

*Terrapin is derived from the Eastern Algonquian word for turtle.
Long considered one of the great American delicacies since colonial times, terrapin
or turtle soup was the standard first course of the elegant society menu throughout
the 18th and 19th centuries. Available from specialty meat and game farms,
turtle has a rich flavor and a delicate texture that is truly unique.*

8 ounces turtle meat or
boneless chicken thighs
Milk, about 2 cups
3 tablespoons butter, divided
1 onion, finely chopped
2 stalks celery, finely chopped
1 teaspoon minced garlic
2½ cups beef stock
1½ cups chopped tomatoes

2 tablespoons freshly squeezed
lemon juice
2 tablespoons dry sherry
1 teaspoon salt
½ teaspoon dried oregano
½ teaspoon freshly ground black pepper
¼ teaspoon dried thyme
1 bay leaf
1 tablespoon all-purpose flour

Cover the turtle meat with the milk. Cover and refrigerate overnight. Drain the turtle and cut into ¼-inch cubes. Discard the milk. In a large saucepan, melt 2 tablespoons of the butter over medium heat. Add the turtle and sauté until lightly browned. With a slotted spoon, transfer the turtle to a bowl and set aside. Add the onion, celery, and garlic to the saucepan and sauté until the vegetables are very tender but not browned. Stir in the reserved turtle, beef stock, tomatoes, lemon juice, sherry, salt, oregano, pepper, thyme, and bay leaf. Bring the mixture to a simmer, then cover the saucepan, reduce the heat to medium-low, and simmer for 1 hour.

In a small bowl, mix the remaining 1 tablespoon of butter and the flour with the back of a fork until smooth. Uncover the saucepan and increase the heat to medium. Whisk the butter and flour mixture into the simmering soup and continue to stir until the soup thickens slightly. Serve immediately.

Serves 6

MAY 26, 1805 — *on my return to the river I passed a
creek about 20 yds. Wide near it's entrance it had a handsome
little stream of running water; in this creek I saw
several softshelled Turtles which were the first that have been
seen this season;* — LEWIS

33

Beef and Barley Soup

*Barley was a staple grain for the early American settlers, providing not only
an excellent addition to soups and stews, but also the basis for many a
fine beverage. So named because of its translucent pearly color, pearl barley
gives this soup its creamy texture.*

3   tablespoons olive oil
1   onion, finely chopped
2   stalks celery, finely chopped
1   carrot, finely chopped
1   leek, white and pale green part only, finely chopped
2   cloves garlic, minced
1½ pounds lean beef, cut into ¼-inch cubes
7   cups beef stock
1   cup pearl barley
    Salt and freshly ground black pepper to taste

In a pot, heat the olive oil over medium heat. Add the onion, celery, carrot, and
leek and sauté until tender. Add the garlic and sauté until fragrant. With a slotted spoon, remove the onion mixture to a bowl and set aside.

Add the meat to the pot and sauté until lightly browned. Stir in the reserved
onion mixture, beef stock, barley, salt, and pepper and bring to a boil. Reduce
the heat to medium-low, cover the pot, and simmer for 1 hour.

Serves 6 to 8

JULY 7, 1806 — *this Spring... contains a very considerable
quantity of water, and actually blubbers with heat for 20 paces
below where it rises. it has every appearance of boiling,
too hot for a man to endure his hand in it 3 seconds. I directd
Sergt. Pryor and John Shields to put each a peice of meat
in the water of different sizes. the one about the size
of my 3 fingers cooked dun in 25 minits the other much thicker
was 32 minits before it became sufficiently dun.* — CLARK

PLATE V

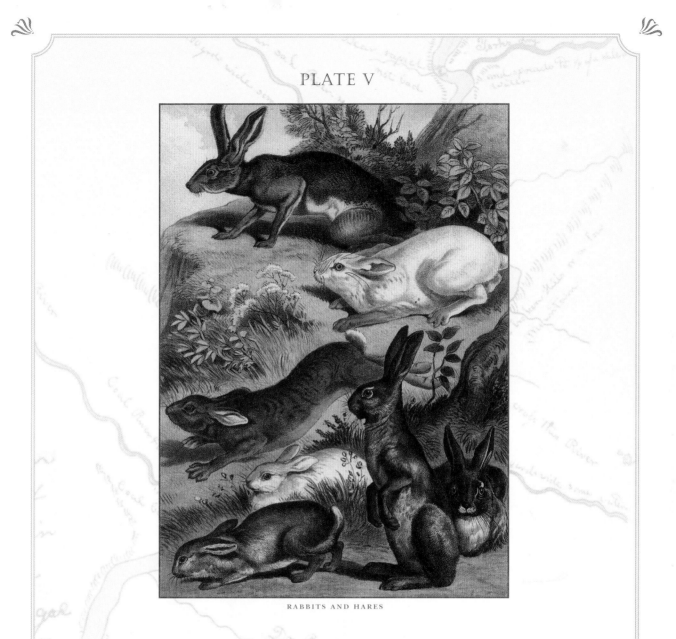

RABBITS AND HARES

FEBRUARY 28, 1806 — *The Hare on this side of the Rocky Mountains is exclusively the inhabitents of the great Plains of the Columbia, as they are of those of the Missouri East of the Mountains. . . . they appear to run with more ease and bound with greater agility than any animal I ever saw. they are extreemly fleet and never burrow or take shelter in the ground when pursued.* — CLARK

Goose and Mushroom Soup with Dumplings

The early American explorers and settlers never wasted anything, so after cooking the Roast Goose with Chestnut and Apple Dressing on page 56, pick off enough meat for this soup and then boil the carcass (starting the bones in cold water) to make the stock. This is also a wonderful way to use leftover Thanksgiving turkey.

¼ cup goose fat or olive oil
1 onion, chopped
1 carrot, sliced
3 cups chopped mushrooms
6 cups goose stock or turkey stock
3 cups chopped cooked
   goose meat or turkey meat
   Salt and freshly ground black
   pepper to taste

Dumplings:
1½ cups all-purpose flour
2 teaspoons baking powder
½ teaspoon salt
3 tablespoons butter
¾ cup milk

In a pot, melt the goose fat over medium heat. Add the onion and carrot and sauté until tender. Add the mushrooms and sauté until tender and most of their liquid has evaporated. Add the goose stock, goose meat, salt, and pepper and bring to a simmer. Cover the pot, reduce heat to medium-low and simmer for 1 hour before adding the dumplings.

For the dumplings: In a bowl, stir together the flour, baking powder, and salt with a fork until blended. Cut in the butter until the mixture resembles coarse meal. Stir in the milk until the dough comes together.

Drop the dough by the heaping tablespoonful into the simmering soup. Cover the pot tightly and continue to cook for 20 minutes. Divide the soup and dumplings into bowls and serve immediately.

Serves 6 to 8

JULY 4, 1804 — *Saw great numbers of Goslings to day which Were nearly grown, the before mentioned Lake is Clear and contain great quantities of fish and Gees & Goslings, The great quantity of those fowl in this Lake induced me to Call it the Gosling Lake,* — CLARK

Cabbage and Beef Soup

The ability to stretch a joint of meat beyond a couple of meals was instrumental to the frugal and sometimes desperate lives of many early Americans. A good roast beef, or boiled tongue could be served the second or third day as a fine soup. Add a cabbage and onion from the root cellar and dinner would be complete. This soup will taste just as good as it did 200 years ago.

       3 tablespoons olive oil
       1 onion, chopped
       8 cups beef stock
       1 green cabbage, chopped
    1½ pounds cooked beef, diced
       1 teaspoon dried dill
       2 teaspoons salt
       1 teaspoon freshly ground black pepper

          Sour cream, for garnish

In a large pot, heat the olive oil over medium heat. Add the onion and sauté until tender. Stir in the beef stock. Add the cabbage, beef, dill, salt, and pepper and bring to a boil. Reduce the heat to medium-low, cover the pot, and simmer for about 2 hours. Serve the soup hot with a dollop of sour cream.

Serves 8

CABBAGE

JUNE 17, 1805 — *The Indian woman much better today; I have still continued the same course of medecine; she is free from pain clear of fever her pulse regular, and eats as heartily as I am willing to permit her of broiled buffaloe well seasoned with pepper and salt and rich soope of the same meat, I think therefore that there is every rational hope of her recovery.* — LEWIS

French Onion Soup

*Among the many things that Thomas Jefferson enjoyed during his residence in Paris
as Ambassador, he most assuredly loved the food and was an adventurous eater
and collector of recipes and cooking methods. Use a good beef stock; if possible make
your own with browned bones, leeks, carrots, and onions.*

3 tablespoons butter
6 cups chopped onions
1 tablespoon water
1½ teaspoons sugar
4 cups beef stock
2 tablespoons brandy
¾ teaspoon salt
¼ teaspoon freshly ground black pepper
4 thick slices of toast
2 cups shredded Gruyère cheese

In a large skillet, melt the butter over medium heat. Stir in the onions and sauté
until tender. Stir in the water and sugar. Reduce the heat to medium-low, cover
the skillet, and cook for about 30 minutes, or until deep golden brown. Stir often, especially towards the end of cooking to make sure that the onions do not
scorch. Add more water if necessary to prevent the onions from scorching.

Preheat the broiler.

Stir the beef stock, brandy, salt, and pepper into the onions and bring to a simmer over medium heat. Continue to simmer for 5 minutes. Ladle the soup into
4 ovenproof bowls. Top each with a piece of toast and divide the Gruyère over
the toast. Place the soup under the broiler until the cheese is bubbly and lightly
browned. Serve immediately.

Serves 4

APRIL 16, 1806 — *The Chief set before me a large platter of
onions which had been sweeted [sweated]. I gave a part of those
onions to all my party and we all eate of them, in this state, the
root is very sweet and the tops tender. the natives requested the
party to dance which they very readily consented and Peter Cruzat
played on the violin and the men danced several dances & retired
to rest in the houses of the 1st. and second Chief.* — CLARK

Corn Chowder

Corn is a uniquely American grain that was bred by the Native American Indians from ancestral grasses. One of the world's first engineered crops, from their individual breeding programs corn was spread throughout North America among the various Indian tribes through trade and barter.

1 tablespoon butter
2 ounces salt pork, finely chopped
1 cup finely chopped onions
4 cups chicken stock
2 cups corn kernels
2 cups diced potatoes
1 cup chopped tomatoes
1 teaspoon salt
1 teaspoon sugar
½ teaspoon freshly ground black pepper
1 cup half-and-half

In a pot, melt the butter over medium heat. Add the salt pork and sauté until lightly browned. Add the onions and sauté until tender. Stir in the chicken stock, corn, potatoes, tomatoes, salt, sugar, and pepper. Simmer, stirring often, until the potatoes are tender. Stir in the half-and-half and heat through.

Serves 8

CORN

AUGUST 22, 1805 — *Gave them a mess of boiled corn which they were fond of. they appear to be verry kind and friendly. We trade with them for dressed mountn. rams Skins and otter Skins &c.* — WHITEHOUSE

Smoked Salmon and Corn Chowder

Chowder, named after the French word chaudière, *or boiling pot, takes its
name from the kettle in which the soup is boiled. A chowder is traditionally a
soup with milk and potatoes. Families ate from the "chowder pot"
that hung from the cast-iron swing-out cooking crane in their fireplaces.
Enjoy this chowder, with slices of warm freshly baked buttered bread.*

6 slices bacon, diced
¼ cup butter
2 onions, chopped
2 stalks celery, chopped
2 cloves garlic, minced
1 teaspoon paprika
1 teaspoon dried tarragon
3 tablespoons all-purpose flour

7 cups milk
4½ cups diced potatoes
2 cups corn kernels
8 ounces smoked salmon, chopped
2 teaspoons freshly squeezed lemon juice
2 teaspoons freshly ground black pepper
2 teaspoons salt

In a large pot, sauté the bacon over medium heat until crisp. Pour out the excess
fat. Add the butter and increase heat to medium-high. Add the onions, celery,
and garlic and sauté until tender. Add the paprika and tarragon. Sprinkle the
flour over the onion mixture and stir with a whisk until the flour is absorbed.
Slowly whisk in 1 cup of the milk until blended. Whisk in the remaining milk.
Stir in the potatoes, corn, smoked salmon, lemon juice, pepper, and salt. Stirring
constantly, bring the chowder just to a boil, then reduce heat to low, and simmer
until the potatoes are tender and the chowder is thick.

Serves 8

OCTOBER 17, 1805 — *I was furnished with a mat to set on, and
one man set about prepareing me something to eate, first he
brought in a piece of Drift log of pine and with a wedge of the
elks horn, and a malet of Stone curioesly carved he Split the log
into Small pieces and lay'd it open on the fire on which he put
round Stones, a woman handed him a basket of water and a
large Salmon about half Dried, when the Stones were hot he put
them in the basket of water with the fish which was soon
sufficently boiled for use it was then taken out put on a platter
of rushes neetly made, and set before me.* — CLARK

MALLARD DUCKS

MARCH 9, 1806 — The Duckinmallard are the same here with those of the U. States . . . [For] the epicures of those parts of the Union where those ducks abound nothing need be added in prais of the exquisit flavor of this duck. I have eaten of them in several parts of the union and I think those of the Columbia equally as delicious. this duck is never found above tide water; we did not meat with them untill after we reached the Marshey Islands; and I believe that they have already left this neighbour-hood, but whether they are gorn Northerly or Southerly, I am unable to deturmine; nor do i know in what part of the country they rais their young. — CLARK

Fish & Fowl

Mussels Steamed with Sweet Herbs

Upon arriving and establishing Fort Clatsop at the western terminus of their voyage, Lewis and Clark found beds of edible mussels growing on the rocks along the Pacific shoreline. Succulent and delicious, steamed mussels pick up the aromas of their steaming liquid and require only fresh bread to dip into the broth.

¼ cup butter, divided
3 shallots, minced
2 cloves garlic, minced
3 cups dry white wine
3 tablespoons minced fresh thyme
4½ pounds mussels, scrubbed and debearded
½ cup chopped Italian parsley
1 tomato, peeled, seeded, and chopped
   Juice of 2 lemons

In a large pot, melt 3 tablespoons of the butter over medium heat. Add the shallots and garlic and sauté until tender. Add the wine and thyme and bring to a boil over high heat. Add the mussels, cover, and steam for about 3 minutes until the mussels open. Discard any unopened mussels. With a slotted spoon, remove the mussels to a large serving bowl. Reduce the heat to medium and whisk the remaining butter into the simmering broth. Stir in the parsley, tomato, and lemon juice and simmer for 5 minutes. Pour the broth over the mussels and serve.

Serves 4

MUSSEL

MARCH 12, 1806 — *the shellfish are the Clam, perrewinkle, common muscle, cockle, and a species with a circular flat shell.*
— CLARK

Cornmeal Crusted Catfish
with Hazelnut Butter

*Today's farmed catfish do not approach the staggering size of those described
by Lewis and Clark, however catfish of any size are still excellent when crispy fried
and served with this tart and rich sauce.*

 4 catfish fillets
    Salt and freshly ground black pepper to taste
¼ cup cornmeal
¼ cup all-purpose flour
 3 tablespoons olive oil
⅓ cup butter
¾ cup chopped hazelnuts
⅓ cup freshly squeezed lemon juice

Season the catfish fillets with the salt and pepper. In a shallow dish, combine the
cornmeal and flour. Dredge the catfish in the cornmeal mixture. In a large skillet, heat the olive oil over medium heat. Add the catfish and cook until golden
brown on both sides and the fish are cooked through. Remove the catfish fillets
to a platter and keep warm.

In a small saucepan, melt the butter over medium heat. Add the hazelnuts and
sauté until fragrant. Stir in the lemon juice.

Spoon the sauce over the fish and serve immediately.

Serves 4

JULY 27, 1804 — *Two of our men last night caught nine catfish
that would together weigh three hundred pounds. The large catfish
are caught in the Missouri with hook and line.* — GASS

Salt Cod Fritters

*Codfish, once salted and dried, can be stored and transported long distances
without refrigeration. Cod was extremely important to the early New England
economy and was widely exported abroad.*

1   pound salt cod
1   pound potatoes, peeled and quartered
2   tablespoons butter
1   egg
½   teaspoon freshly ground black pepper
    Oil for frying

Place the salt cod in a bowl and cover with cold water. Cover the bowl and refrigerate overnight.

Drain the cod and set aside.

In a large saucepan, cover the potatoes with water and bring to a boil. Reduce the heat to medium and cook until the potatoes are tender. With a slotted spoon, transfer the potatoes to a bowl. Add the butter and mash the potatoes until smooth.

Add the salt cod to the simmering potato water and simmer until the fish just flakes. Drain and transfer the fish to a cutting board. Discard any bones or skin. Chop the cod then add it to the potatoes. Add the egg and pepper. Stir together vigorously until well blended.

In a deep fryer or large heavy skillet, heat 3 inches of oil to 375 degrees. In batches, carefully drop a heaping tablespoon of the cod mixture into the hot oil. Cook for about 4 minutes, or until golden brown on all sides. Drain on paper towels. Serve hot.

Serves 6 to 8

AUGUST 20, 1805 — *the Chief further informed me that he had understood from the persed nose Indians who inhabit this river below the rocky mountains that it ran a great way toward the seting sun and finally lost itself in a great lake of water which was illy taisted, and where the white men lived.* — LEWIS

PLATE VI

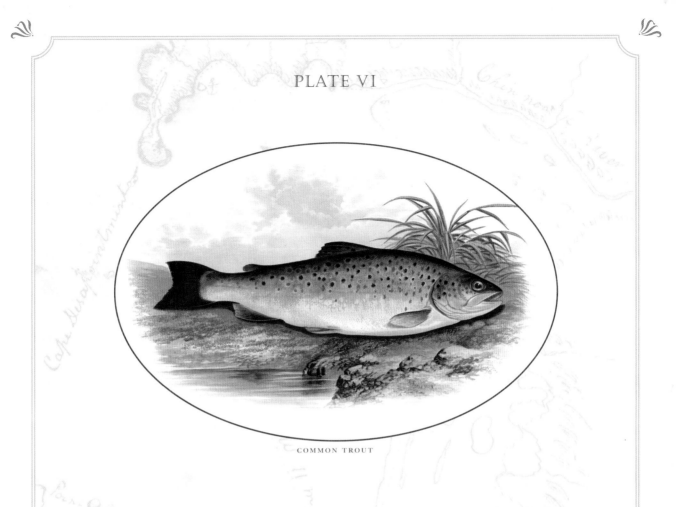

COMMON TROUT

JUNE 13, 1805 — Goodrich had caught a half a douzen very fine trout and a number of both species of the white fish. these trout are from sixteen to twenty three inches in length, precisely resemble our mountain or speckled trout in form and the position of their fins, but the specks on these are of a deep black instead of the red or goald colour of those common to the U'. States. these are furnished long sharp teeth on the pallet and tongue and have generally a small dash of red on each side behind the front ventral fins; the flesh is of a pale yellowish red, or when in good order, of a rose red. — LEWIS

Sole with Browned Butter and Caper Sauce

Sole belongs to the group of fish known as flounder, all characterized by having a broad, flat body, and both eyes on one side of their head. Select medium-sized fillets for this simple and elegant meal.

  4 sole fillets
      Salt and freshly ground black pepper to taste
      All-purpose flour for dredging
  2 tablespoons butter

Browned Butter and Caper Sauce:
  ¼ cup butter
  ¼ cup dry white wine
  1 tablespoon freshly squeezed lemon juice
  2 tablespoons capers

Season the sole fillets with salt and pepper. Dredge lightly in the flour and shake off the excess. In a large skillet, melt the 2 tablespoons of butter over medium-high heat. Add the sole and cook for about 3 minutes per side. Remove the sole to a platter.

For the sauce: Add the remaining ¼ cup of the butter to the hot skillet. Let the butter cook for about 2 minutes, or until it stops sizzling and turns golden brown. Whisk in the wine and lemon juice and simmer until the liquid has reduced by half. Stir in the capers and pour the sauce over the sole. Serve immediately.

Serves 4

MARCH 13, 1806 — *The flounder is also an inhabitant of the salt water. we have seen them also on the beach where they had been left by the tide. The Indians eat the latter and esteem it very fine. these several species are the same with those of the Atlantic coast.* — LEWIS

Salmon Quenelles with Sorrel Sauce

*Popular in England and Europe as an accompaniment to lamb and beef,
this lighter version of sorrel sauce is strong enough to stand up to salmon but won't
overpower it. These light pink quenelles, or dumplings, make an elegant main
course served on buttered points of toast with steamed asparagus.*

Salmon Quenelles:
- 1 pound skinless salmon fillet, all bones removed
- 1 tablespoon butter
- 2 shallots, minced
- 2 slices white bread, crusts removed
- 1 egg white
- 1 teaspoon salt
- ¼ teaspoon freshly ground black pepper
- 1¼ cups heavy cream

Sorrel Sauce:
- ½ cup butter
- 1 tablespoon freshly squeezed lemon juice
- 2 egg yolks
- 2 tablespoons finely chopped fresh sorrel

Cut the salmon into ½-inch cubes and place in the freezer for 15 minutes.

In a small skillet, melt the butter over medium heat. Add the shallots and sauté until tender. With a rubber spatula, transfer the shallots and butter to the bowl of a food processor or blender. Add the chilled salmon, bread, egg white, salt, and pepper and process just until smooth. With the motor running, pour in the cream and purée just until combined with the salmon.

Bring a pot of salted water to a simmer over medium heat.

To shape the quenelles: Take a serving spoon that will hold about 3 tablespoons of the salmon mixture and dip it in water. Scoop up a spoonful of the mixture. Take a second serving spoon, and use the bowl of the spoon to form a rounded top on the mixture in the first spoon. Then take the second spoon, and use it to loosen the quenelle from the first spoon and transfer the mixture gently into the simmering water. Do not crowd the quenelles in the pot. Cook the quenelles, turning them once, for about 7 minutes. With a slotted spoon, carefully transfer the cooked quenelles to a plate covered with paper towels to drain. Keep warm in a 200-degree oven.

For the sorrel sauce: In a saucepan, melt the butter and lemon juice together over low heat. Whisk in the egg yolks, increase the heat to medium-low, and continue to whisk until the mixture just begins to thicken. Whisk in the sorrel and serve immediately with the quenelles.

Serves 6

SALMON

OCTOBER 19, 1805 — *the Natives came to See us in their canoes. brought us Some fish which had been roasted and pounded up fine and made up in balls, which eat verry well.* — WHITEHOUSE

Grilled Maple-Glazed Salmon

*Upon arriving at the Columbia River, Lewis and Clark relished the
abundant salmon after a year of venison, bear, and other game. In some places
at certain seasons the salmon were reputed to be running so densely they could
be walked upon, or so it has been reported.*

¼ cup maple syrup
2 tablespoons Dijon mustard
2 tablespoons brown sugar
2 tablespoons melted butter
1 (2-pound) salmon fillet, skinned and small bones removed
  Salt and freshly ground black pepper to taste

In a bowl, whisk together the maple syrup, Dijon mustard, brown sugar, and
melted butter. Season the salmon fillet with the salt and pepper.

Prepare a hot charcoal fire. Spread half of the maple syrup mixture on top of the
salmon and let stand at room temperature for 30 minutes. Transfer the salmon
to the grill and cook until the fish just flakes. Brush the salmon with the remaining maple syrup glaze during cooking.

Serves 6

AUGUST 13, 1805 — *...on my return to my lodge an indian
called me into his bower and gave me a small morsel of the flesh
of an antelope boiled, and a peice of a fresh salmon roasted,
both which I eat with a very good relish. this was the first
salmon I had seen and perfectly convinced me that we were on
the waters of the Pacific Ocean.* — LEWIS

PLATE VII

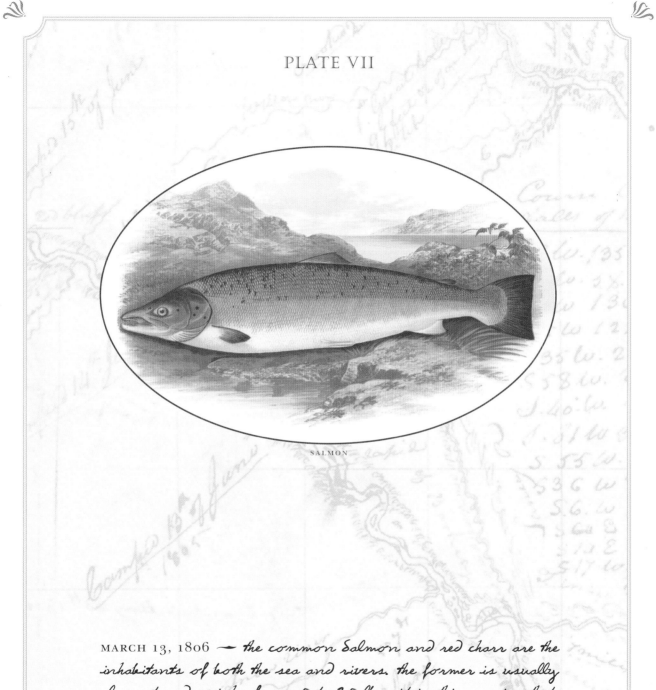

SALMON

MARCH 13, 1806 — the common Salmon and red charr are the inhabitants of both the sea and rivers. the former is usually largest and weighs from 5 to 15 lbs. it is this species that extends itself into all the rivers and little creeks on this side of the continent, and to which the natives are so much indebted for their subsistence. — LEWIS

VII

Alder-Smoked Trout

Alder is a type of birch that commonly grows in the colder climates of northern latitudes. Alder grows all over New England and was the preferred wood for smoking during the 18th and 19th centuries. Enjoy these smoked trout either alone with a bit of horseradish, some salt water crackers and a cold beer, or use the meat in other dishes including the Smoked Trout Cakes on page 50.

  3 cups water
  1 cup dry white wine
 ⅓ cup sugar
 ¼ cup noniodized salt
 ½ teaspoon freshly ground black pepper
  4 pounds whole cleaned trout

    Two pans of alder chips

In a large stainless steel or glass bowl, combine the water, wine, sugar, salt, and pepper. Stir until the sugar and salt dissolve. Place the whole trout in the brine and weigh down with a plate to completely submerge the trout. Cover with plastic wrap and refrigerate 24 hours.

Remove the trout from the brine and rinse lightly. Prop the body cavity open with two toothpicks. Place the trout on a rack and allow to air dry for 1 hour.

Lightly oil the racks in the smoker. Place the trout on the racks. Use 2 pans of woodchips. Smoke the trout for about 6 to 8 hours depending on the thickness of the trout.

JANUARY 17, 1806 — *Their wooden bowls and troughs are of different forms and sizes, and most generally dug out of a solid piece; . . . these are extreemely well executed and many of them neatly carved, the larger vessels with hand-holes to them; in these vessels they boil their fish or flesh by means of hot stones which they immerce in the water with the article to be boiled.* — LEWIS

Smoked Trout Cakes

*The clear cold waters of North America seethed with an abundance of fish.
Lewis and Clark described five new species of salmon and trout during
their voyage of discovery.*

¼ cup mayonnaise
1 egg
3 tablespoons minced scallions
2 tablespoons prepared horseradish
1 tablespoon minced fresh dill
1 tablespoon freshly squeezed lemon juice
¼ teaspoon freshly ground white pepper
1 pound Alder-Smoked Trout meat, see page 49
1 cup fresh bread crumbs

  About 3 cups fresh bread crumbs for dredging

¼ cup butter

In a large bowl, whisk together the mayonnaise, egg, scallions, horseradish, dill,
lemon juice, and white pepper until blended. Stir in the trout and 1 cup of the
fresh bread crumbs together until well combined. Do not overmix. Form the
mixture into 8 patties. Place the 3 cups of bread crumbs in a shallow dish.
Dredge the cakes in the bread crumbs. Place the cakes on a baking sheet, cover,
and chill for 1 hour.

In a large skillet, melt the butter over medium heat. Add the trout cakes and
cook for about 4 minutes per side until nicely browned. Serve immediately.

Serves 4 as a main course or 8 as a first course

OCTOBER 26, 1805 — *our hunters returned in the evening
Killed five Deer, four verry large grey Squirels and a grouse.
One of the guard at the river gigged a Salmon Trout, which we
had fried in a little Bears oil which the Chief we passed below the
narrows gave us: this I thought one of the most delicious fish
I have ever tasted* — CLARK

Anchovy Essence

*This is the recipe from which Worcestershire sauce later evolved.
The history of anchovy sauces can be traced back to the garum fish sauces of
the Roman Empire, and were a standard at the more affluent American table.*

1 cup water
½ cup cider vinegar
¼ cup molasses
¼ cup dry red wine
¼ cup minced shallots
2 ounces anchovies, drained and finely chopped
1 teaspoon finely minced lemon zest
⅛ teaspoon dried hot chile flakes
1 whole clove

In a small saucepan, combine all the ingredients and bring to a boil. Reduce the heat to medium-low, cover the saucepan, and simmer for 1 hour. Remove the lid and simmer for an additional 15 minutes. Set aside and let the mixture cool completely. Strain the cooled mixture through a fine sieve and discard the solids. Store covered in the refrigerator for up to one month.

Makes about ½ cup

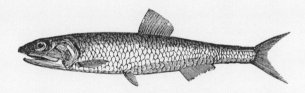

ANCHOVY

MARCH 4, 1806 — *we live sumptuously on our wappetoe and sturgeon. the Anchovy is so delicate that they soon become tainted unless pickled or smoked. the natives run a small stick through their gills and hang them in the smoke of their lodges, or kindle a small fire under them for the purpose of drying them.* — LEWIS

Chicken Capitolade

Often served at Monticello as a breakfast dish, this hash is also an excellent choice for a luncheon or light supper. Select a fine dry wine to cook with, and serve the balance of the wine with the meal. Serve over toast or mashed potatoes.

2 tablespoons butter
3 tablespoons minced onion
1 tablespoon minced shallot
1 clove garlic, minced
3 cups sliced mushrooms
1 tablespoon all-purpose flour
⅓ cup dry white wine
1 cup chicken stock
2 cups diced cooked chicken
½ teaspoon salt
½ teaspoon dried tarragon
¼ teaspoon freshly ground black pepper
1 cup peas

In a cast-iron skillet, melt the butter over medium heat. Add the onion and shallot and sauté until tender. Add the garlic and sauté until fragrant. Add the mushrooms and sauté until tender. Sprinkle the flour over the mushroom mixture and stir until it is evenly absorbed. Stir in the white wine and bring to a simmer. Stir in the chicken stock and bring to a simmer. Stir in the chicken, salt, tarragon, and pepper and simmer until the mixture has slightly thickened. Stir in the peas and heat through before serving.

Serves 4

TARRAGON

OCTOBER 11, 1809 — *The tarragon you were so kind as to send me is now growing with the former bunch.*

— JEFFERSON to William Thornton

PLATE VIII

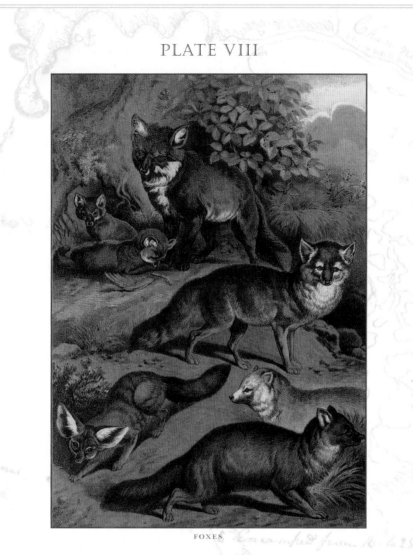

FOXES

MAY 31, 1805 — I saw near those bluffs the most beautifull fox that I ever beheld, the colours appeared to me to be a fine orrange yellow, white and black; I endevoured to kill this anamal but it discovered me at a considerable distance, and finding that I could get no nearer, I fired on him as he ran, and missed him; he concealed himself under the rocks of the clift; it appeared to me to be about the size of the common red fox of the Atlantic states, or reather smaller than the large fox common to this country; convinced I am that it is a distinct species. — LEWIS

VIII

Chicken Stuffed with Figs

Figs are among the world's oldest domesticated fruits. Figs began their cultivation throughout the warm regions of the Old World and were eagerly repatriated to the New World. Thomas Jefferson experimented with many varieties at Monticello with the earliest entry in his Farm Book of a "dº (dozen) of figs" planted in 1769, fully seven years before the War of Independence.

3   tablespoons butter, softened
1   teaspoon salt
½   teaspoon freshly ground black pepper
¼   teaspoon ground ginger
1   roasting chicken
1   cup dried figs
1   onion, chopped
¼   cup Madeira

Preheat oven to 375 degrees. Lightly oil a roasting pan.

In a small bowl, combine the butter, salt, pepper, and ginger with a fork. Rub the chicken inside and out with the mixture. Stuff the cavity with the figs, then truss with string. Place the chopped onion in the bottom of the roasting pan. Place the chicken on top of the onions. Roast the chicken for about 1 hour, or until the juices run clear when the chicken is pierced with a skewer in the thigh. Remove the chicken to a serving platter and let rest 10 minutes before carving. Place the roasting pan on top of stove over medium-high heat, whisking up any browned bits. When hot, deglaze the pan with the Madeira and reduce by one-half, whisking constantly. Strain the sauce and serve with the chicken.

Serves 6

DECEMBER 28, 1794 — *I ever wish to have opportunity of enjoying your society, knowing your fondness for figs, I have daily wished you could have partaken of ours this year. I never saw so great a crop & they are still abundant. of three kinds which I brought from France, there is one, of which I have a single bush, superior to any fig I ever tasted anywhere.*

— JEFFERSON to George Wyeth

Creamed Turkey with Corn and Bacon over Polenta

At one time suggested by Benjamin Franklin for the national symbol of the United States, the turkey is another American original. Supplanted by the eagle as the national bird, the turkey still takes center stage every Thanksgiving Day. There will usually be sufficient leftovers from a roast turkey to create this delicious and hearty main course. Polenta, known to the colonists as corn meal mush, would be simmered slowly in front of a wood fire while the bacon was frying in a cast-iron "spider," a skillet with three legs set directly upon the coals.

6 slices bacon, chopped
2 cups corn kernels
2 cups cooked diced turkey
2 tablespoons butter
1 tablespoon all-purpose flour
¾ cup heavy cream
¾ cup milk
1 cup chopped tomatoes
1 teaspoon salt
½ teaspoon freshly ground black pepper
3 tablespoons chopped fresh basil

Polenta:
4 cups turkey stock
1 teaspoon salt
1 cup cornmeal
6 ounces (about 1½ cups) diced fontina cheese
¼ cup freshly grated Parmesan cheese

In a large skillet, cook the bacon over medium heat until crisp. Add the corn and turkey and sauté until the corn is cooked through. Remove the mixture from the skillet to a bowl and set aside.

Add the butter to the skillet. Sprinkle the flour into the skillet and whisk until blended and bubbly. Slowly add the cream and the milk in a thin stream, whisking constantly. Simmer, continuing to whisk, until the mixture has slightly thickened. Stir in the reserved turkey mixture, tomatoes, salt, and pepper. Reduce the heat to medium-low and simmer until heated through. Stir in the basil and keep warm over low heat.

For the polenta: In a large heavy saucepan, combine the turkey stock and salt. Bring to a boil over medium-high heat. Whisking constantly, slowly add the corn meal a little at a time. Reduce heat to medium and continue whisking until mixture has slightly thickened. Remove the saucepan from the heat and stir in the fontina and Parmesan.

Serves 4

TURKEY

AUGUST 24, 1805 — *the party had killed several phesents and cought a fiew Small fish on which they had Subsisted in my absence. also a heath hen near the size of a Small turkey.* — CLARK

Roast Goose with Chestnut and Apple Dressing and Giblet Gravy

Three years before the War of Independence, Thomas Jefferson used the American common chestnut as the rootstock upon which he grafted the French chestnut in his Monticello garden to yield a tastier nut meat. Chestnuts give a rich flavor and texture to this incomparable stuffing. After enjoying this succulent meal, be sure to save all the bones and extra meat to use to make the Goose and Mushroom Soup on page 35.

Chestnut and Apple Dressing:
20 whole chestnuts
2½ cups ½-inch bread cubes, lightly toasted
1 cup finely chopped apples
1 tablespoon minced fresh parsley
1 tablespoon minced shallot
1 teaspoon salt
½ teaspoon freshly ground black pepper
¼ cup melted butter
½ cup heavy cream

1 goose, about 8 to 10 pounds
Salt and freshly ground black pepper to taste

Giblet Gravy:
Goose giblets
Water
¼ cup all-purpose flour
¼ cup heavy cream

Preheat oven to 325 degrees.

For the dressing: With a sharp paring knife, score each chestnut with an X on the flat side of the chestnut. Place the chestnuts in a saucepan and cover them with water. Bring to a boil, then reduce the heat to medium-low, and simmer for 25 minutes. Drain the chestnuts and remove the shell and bitter membrane. Chop the chestnuts and spread them out on a baking sheet. Toast in the oven for about 7 minutes.

In a large bowl, toss together the chestnuts, toasted bread cubes, apples, parsley, shallot, salt, and pepper. Drizzle the melted butter over the mixture and toss lightly to evenly distribute the butter. Pour the cream over the mixture and toss to coat.

Remove and reserve the giblets from the goose. Season the inside of the cavity of the goose with salt and pepper. Stuff the dressing into the cavity of the goose. Truss the goose with kitchen string. Place the goose in a roasting pan and season with salt and pepper. Roast the goose, basting often with the pan juices, for about 2½ hours, or until the juices run clear when the goose is pierced with a skewer in the thigh.

For the gravy: In a saucepan, combine the reserved giblets and enough water to cover them. Bring to a boil, then reduce the heat to medium-low and simmer for 2 hours. Strain the giblets and measure the broth. If there is more than 2 cups of broth, return the broth to the saucepan and simmer until the broth is reduced to 2 cups. Set aside.

Remove the goose to a platter and tent with foil to keep warm. Remove all but ¼ cup of the goose fat from the roasting pan. Place the roasting pan on the stovetop over medium heat. Sprinkle the flour over the fat in the pan and whisk until smooth and bubbly. Slowly add the reserved broth in a thin stream, whisking constantly. Continue to cook, whisking constantly, until the gravy has thickened. Whisk in the cream until heated through. Transfer the gravy to a gravy boat and serve with the goose and dressing.

Serves 6

CANADA GEESE

APRIL 14, 1805 — *Saw many gees feeding on the tender grass in the praries and several of their nests in trees; we have not in a single instance found the nest of this bird in or near the ground.* — LEWIS

Duck Breasts with Pear Eau de Vie Sauce

Eau de vie is the simple distilled essence of fermented pears or other fruits.
The alcohol evaporates during cooking, leaving its flavor behind to lend a layer
of richness to this incredibly savory and delicious dish. During the late 18th and
early 19th centuries many Americans, including Thomas Jefferson,
distilled their own spirits.

1 cup diced dried pears
½ cup pear eau de vie
1 tablespoon olive oil
¼ cup minced shallots
¼ cup water
½ cup heavy cream
  Salt and freshly ground black pepper to taste
4 duck breasts

In a small bowl, combine the dried pears and the eau de vie. Cover and let stand for 1 hour.

In a saucepan, heat the olive oil over medium heat. Add the shallots and sauté until tender. Add the pears and their liquid and sauté for 1 minute. Stir in the water and bring to a simmer. Reduce the heat to medium-low, cover the saucepan, and simmer for 10 minutes. Stir in the cream and simmer for an additional 10 minutes, or until the sauce has slightly thickened. Season with salt and pepper and keep warm over low heat.

Preheat the broiler. Lightly oil a broiling pan.

Place the duck breasts, skin-side up, on the prepared broiling pan. Season the duck with salt and pepper. Broil until the duck is done but still pink inside. Place the duck breasts on a serving platter and spoon the sauce over them before serving.

Serves 4

NOV. 26, 1792 — *... I am to carry on the business, proposing nothing more than the distillation of my own grain & fruit ...* — JEFFERSON to George Divers

PLATE IX

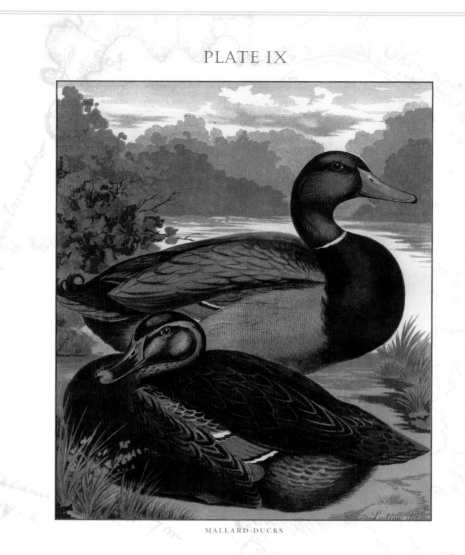

MALLARD DUCKS

MARCH 9, 1806 — [For] the epicures of those parts of the Union where those Ducks abound nothing need be added in prais of the exquisit flavor of this duck. I have eaten of them in several parts of the union and I think those of the Columbia equally as delicious. this duck is never found above tide water; we did not meat with them untill after we reached the Marshey Islands; and I believe that they have already left this neighbourhood, but whether they are gorn Northerly or Southerly, I am unable to deturmine; nor do I know in what part of the country they rais their young. — CLARK

Roast Duck with Blackberry Sauce

*Berries that weren't eaten ripe from the vine or made into delicious jams,
pies and jellies, went into a sauce like this one, to grace the Sunday dinner table.
Ducks have all dark meat due to the large amount of myoglobin in their muscles.
The rich dark meat is complemented by the tart dark sauce.*

1 duck, about 4 pounds
   Salt and freshly ground black pepper to taste

Blackberry Sauce:
   2 tablespoons butter
   1 shallot, minced
   2 tablespoons red wine vinegar
   1 tablespoon sugar
1¼ cups strained blackberry purée from about 2 cups fresh blackberries
   ¼ cup duck stock or chicken stock

Preheat oven to 350 degrees.

Season the duck inside and outside with salt and pepper. Transfer to a roasting pan. Roast for about 1 hour, or until the juices run clear when the thigh is pierced. Let the duck rest for 15 minutes before carving.

For the sauce: In a small saucepan, melt the butter over medium heat. Add the shallot and sauté until tender. Whisk in the vinegar and sugar and simmer until the liquid has almost evaporated. Whisk in the blackberry purée, duck stock, salt, and pepper and simmer until the sauce has reduced to about 1 cup. Serve the sauce spooned over the carved duck.

Serves 4

JULY 30, 1805 — *by this time it was getting nearly dark and a duck lit on the shore in about 40 steps of me and I killed it, having now secured my supper I looked our for a suitable place to amuse myself in combating the musquetoes for the ballance of the evening.* — LEWIS

MOOSE STALKED BY GRIZZLIES

JULY 15, 1806 — ...McNeal returned with his musquet broken off at the breach and informed me that...he had approached a white bear within ten feet without discover[ing] him the bear being in the thick brush, the horse took the allarm and turning short threw him...under the bear; this animal raised himself on his hinder feet for battle, and gave him time to recover from his fall...and with his clubbed musquet he struck the bear over the head and cut him, the bear stunned... fell to the ground; ...this gave McNeal time to climb a willow tree... and thus made his escape. — LEWIS

Meats

Home Corned Beef

Fresh meat generally spoils after only a few days without refrigeration or some kind of preservation. However meat laid in a salt brine for several weeks can be stored much longer. This process, known as corning, allowed members of the Corps of Discovery, to maintain a supply of edible meat throughout the cold months of winter.

4 quarts warm water	*For the Corned Beef:*
2 cups noniodized salt	2 onions, sliced
¼ cup sugar	2 cloves garlic, minced
2 tablespoons pickling spice	2 bay leaves
1 teaspoon saltpeter (optional)	6 whole cloves
5 pounds fresh beef brisket	

In a large nonreactive pot, whisk together the warm water, salt, sugar, pickling spice, and saltpeter (if used) until the salt has dissolved. Place the brisket in the brine and weigh down with a plate. The beef must be completely submerged. Cover the pot and refrigerate for 3 weeks. Turn the brisket every 5 days.

After 3 weeks remove the brisket from the brine and rinse well. Discard the brine. The corned beef is now ready to be cooked.

Remove the corned beef from the brine and rinse thoroughly. Place the corned beef in a large pot and barely cover with water. Add the onions, garlic, bay leaves, and cloves. Bring to a boil, then reduce heat to medium-low, cover pot, and simmer for 2½ hours. To serve, slice the meat across the grain.

Serves 8 to 10

JANUARY 5, 1806 — *they commenced the making of salt and found that they could obtain from 3 quarts to a gallon a day; they brought with them a specemine of the salt of about a gallon, we found it excellent, fine, strong, & white; this was a great treat to myself and most of the party, having not had any since the 20th Ult mo; I say most of the party, for my friend Capt Clark declares it to be a mear matter of indifference with him whether he uses it or not, for myself I must confess I felt a considerable inconvenience from the want of it.* — LEWIS

Grilled Rib-Eye Steaks
with Horseradish and Anchovy Butter

*Probably the least commonly consumed meat during colonial times was beef.
Although this traditional and delicious compound butter tastes best with the
homemade Anchovy Essence on page 51, you can substitute Worcestershire sauce
instead. Use mesquite charcoal to grill the meat. It burns hotter than most
other charcoals and is best for grilling.*

Horseradish and Anchovy Butter:
- 4 tablespoons butter, softened
- 2 tablespoons prepared horseradish
- 4 teaspoons Anchovy Essence, see page 51, or Worcestershire sauce
- ½ teaspoon salt

- 6 rib-eye steaks
   Salt and freshly ground black pepper to taste

For the butter: In a small bowl, combine the butter, horseradish, anchovy essence,
and salt. Mash together with the back of a fork until well blended. Place the mixture on a piece of plastic wrap and form into a log about 3 inches long. Chill at
least 1 hour, or until firm. Cut into 6 slices and keep chilled.

Prepare the grill. Season the steaks with salt and pepper. Grill the steaks over a
hot fire for 4 to 6 minutes per side for medium rare. Divide the steaks onto 6
plates and top with a slice of horseradish and anchovy butter.

Serves 6

SEPTEMBER 20, 1806 — *we saw some cows on the bank
which was a joyfull Sight to the party and caused a
Shout to be raised for joy. . .* — CLARK

Kentucky Bourbon Stew

Named after Bourbon County, Kentucky, where much of the whiskey was produced, bourbon whiskey has been produced since 1775. The alcohol evaporates during the preparation of this fine stew, leaving only a hint of its flavor behind.

2 pounds oxtails
2 pounds meaty short ribs
  Salt and freshly ground black pepper to taste
  All-purpose flour
½ cup olive oil
1 onion, chopped
2 tablespoons minced garlic
½ cup Kentucky bourbon
4 cups beef stock
1 bay leaf
½ teaspoon dried thyme

Preheat oven to 350 degrees.

Season the oxtails and short ribs well with salt and pepper. Lightly dredge the meat in the flour and shake off the excess. In a Dutch oven, heat the olive oil over medium-high heat. Add the meat and brown well on all sides. Add the onion and garlic and sauté until tender. Stir in the bourbon, scraping up any browned bits. Take care that the bourbon does not flame up; if it does cover the pot with a lid to smother the flames. Stir in the stock, bay leaf, and thyme. Bring the mixture to a simmer, then cover the pot, and cook in the oven for 3 hours. Remove from the oven and skim off any fat. Taste for seasoning and serve.

Serves 4 to 6

JANUARY 1, 1805 — *Two shots were fired from the swivel, followed by a round of small arms, to welcome the New year. Captain Lewis then gave each a glass of good old whiskey; and a short time after another was given by Captain Clarke.* — GASS

PLATE X

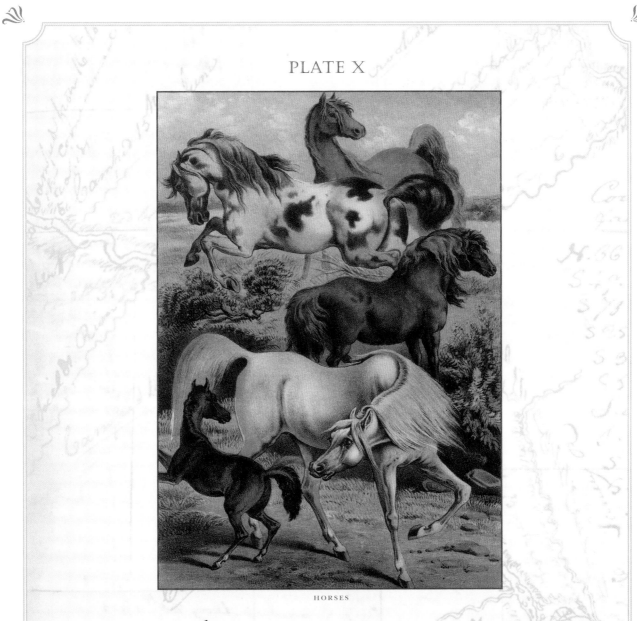

HORSES

APRIL 28, 1806 — *This morning early Yellept brought a very eligant white horse to our camp and presented him to Capt. C. signifying his wish to get a kettle but on being informed that we had already disposed of every kettle we could possible spear he said he was content with whatever he thought proper to give him. Capt. C. gave him his sword (for which he had expressed a great desire) a hundred balls and powder and some s[m]all articles with which he appeared perfectly satisfyied.* — LEWIS

Braised Brisket with Mushrooms and Onions

*Brisket comes from the front or chest of the cow or game animal and lends itself
particularly well to long braising. Generally used for corned beef,
the brisket is surprisingly versatile.*

1	cup dried wild mushrooms, such as morels, chanterelles, or porcini
2½	cups boiling water
¼	cup olive oil, divided
2	onions, chopped
12	ounces button mushrooms, sliced
2	cloves garlic, minced
1	tablespoon red wine vinegar
3	pounds beef brisket
	Salt and freshly ground black pepper to taste
2	cups dry red wine
2	bay leaves
1	teaspoon dried thyme

Preheat oven to 400 degrees.

Place the dried mushrooms in a bowl. Pour the boiling water over the mushrooms and let stand until cool. With a slotted spoon, transfer the mushrooms to a cutting board. Strain the mushroom soaking liquid through a fine sieve lined with a double layer of moistened cheesecloth and discard the solids. Set aside the strained mushroom liquid. Finely chop the mushrooms and set aside.

In a Dutch oven, heat 2 tablespoons of the olive oil over medium heat. Add the onions and sauté until tender. Add the button mushrooms and sauté until tender and most of the liquid has evaporated. Add the reserved wild mushrooms, garlic, and vinegar and sauté until most of the liquid has evaporated. Transfer the mushroom mixture to a bowl and return the Dutch oven to the stovetop. Add the remaining 2 tablespoons of olive oil. Season the brisket with salt and pepper and brown well on all sides. Pour in the red wine, reserved mushroom liquid, reserved mushroom mixture, bay leaves, and thyme and bring to a simmer. Cover the Dutch oven and place in the oven. Cook for about 3 hours, or until the brisket is very tender.

Transfer the brisket to a cutting board and let rest for 10 minutes before carving. Place the Dutch oven on the stovetop and reduce the sauce if it is too liquid. Slice the brisket across the grain and arrange on a serving platter. Spoon the sauce over and serve.

Serves 6 to 8

THE AMERICAN ELK, OR WAPITI

FEBRUARY 7, 1806 — *This evening we had what I call an excellent supper it consisted of a piece of marrowbone, a piece of brisket of boiled elk that had the appearance of a little fat on it. This for Fort Clatsop is liveing in high stile, and in fact fiesting.* — CLARK

Frizzled Beef

"Frizzled" is a 19th century word that means "fried until crisp and curled."
This recipe calls for "dried" beef, a variation on beef jerky or the Indian staple
pemmican. Also known as chipped beef, it can generally be found in
grocery stores sealed in a clear glass bottle.

5   ounces dried beef
¼   cup butter
3   tablespoons all-purpose flour
2   cups milk
½   teaspoon Anchovy Essence, see page 51, or Worcestershire sauce
¼   teaspoon freshly ground black pepper

Buttermilk Biscuits, see page 102

Rinse the dried beef in a colander and let drain. Coarsely chop the beef. In a cast-iron skillet, melt the butter over medium heat. Add the beef and sauté until the beef is crispy on the edges. With a slotted spoon, remove the beef and set aside. Sprinkle the flour into the skillet and whisk until blended and bubbly. Slowly add the milk in a thin stream, whisking constantly. Simmer, whisking constantly, until the mixture has slightly thickened. Stir in the anchovy essence, pepper, and reserved beef. Heat through and serve over Buttermilk Biscuits.

Serves 4

APRIL 6, 1806 — *This morning we had the dryed meat secured in skins and the canoes loaded,* — LEWIS

Beef Jerky

*Smoke drying game as large as a whole elk or buffalo occupied several days.
However, once dried, jerky could sustain the men for days until the next successful
hunt. Jerky was used plain, or mixed with berries and animal fat to form pemmican.
The recipe is designed to use the Luhr-Jensen smoker, but if you have a different
model, you might need to vary the amount of smoke and the cooking time.*

2 pounds sirloin tip roast

2 cups water
¼ cup noniodized salt
2 tablespoons sugar
1 clove garlic, minced
½ teaspoon freshly ground black pepper

1 pan mesquite or hickory chips

Remove all fat from the beef. To facilitate slicing, partially freeze the meat before
slicing. Slice the meat across the grain as thinly as possible.

In a large bowl, stir together the water, salt, sugar, garlic, and pepper until the
salt has dissolved. Add the sliced meat and let it soak in the brine for 45 minutes.
Remove the meat from the brine and rinse in fresh water.

Lightly oil the racks in the smoker. Drape the meat over the racks. Use 1 pan of
woodchips. Smoke the meat for about 12 to 15 hours depending on the thickness of the meat. The beef jerky should be dry but still slightly pliable.

JANUARY 16, 1806 — *This evening we finished curing the
meat. . .we have plenty of Elk beef for the present and a little
salt, our houses dry and comfortable, and having made up our
minds to remain until the 1ˢᵗ of April, every one appears
content with his situation and his fare.* — LEWIS

PLATE XI

BISON ATTACKED BY WOLVES

MAY 5, 1805 — we scarcely see a gang of buffaloe without observing a parsel of those faithfull shepherds on their skirts in readiness to take care of the maimed wounded. the large wolf never barks, but howls as those of the atlantic states do. — LEWIS

Veal Croquettes

*The delicacy and unique flavor of veal, be it from beef or buffalo, made it
especially welcome at the finest tables in Jefferson's America as well as
to frontiersmen far from civilization.*

1 egg
2 tablespoons finely minced onion
1 tablespoon finely minced fresh parsley
1 teaspoon salt
¼ teaspoon freshly ground black pepper
1½ pounds ground veal
½ cup fresh bread crumbs

Coating:
   All-purpose flour
1 egg
1 tablespoon water
2 cups fresh bread crumbs

   Oil for frying

In a bowl, whisk together the egg, onion, parsley, salt, and pepper. Add the veal
and the ½ cup of bread crumbs and mix together gently but thoroughly. With
your hands, shape into small ovals.

For the coating: Place the flour in a shallow dish. Whisk the egg and water in a separate shallow dish. Place the 2 cups of bread crumbs in a separate shallow dish.
Lightly dust the croquettes in the flour. Dip in the egg mixture, then dredge
with the bread crumbs. Place the croquettes on a baking sheet. Cover with plastic wrap and chill in the refrigerator for 1 hour.

In a large skillet, heat 1 inch of oil over medium-high heat. Add the croquettes
and fry until golden brown on all sides. Remove the croquettes with a slotted
spoon and drain on paper towels. Serve immediately.

Serves 6

MAY 14, 1805 — *I felt an inclination to eat some veal and
walked on shore and killed a very fine buffaloe calf...* — LEWIS

Charbonneau's Boudin Blanc Terrine

The French influence on America's cuisine began even before the purchase of the Louisiana Territory. Toussaint Charbonneau, guide, interpreter, and husband to Sacagawea, was renowned for his boudin blanc. The other members of the Corps of Discovery considered it a particularly special treat when he found the time and ingredients to make it.

Spiced Cream:
1½ cups heavy cream
2 onions, chopped
2 shallots, chopped
2 cloves garlic, minced
5 teaspoons salt
1 teaspoon whole black peppercorns
⅛ teaspoon ground nutmeg
⅛ teaspoon dried thyme

2 tablespoons butter
⅓ cup minced shallots
1 pound center pork loin, cut into ½-inch cubes and chilled
3 eggs
¼ cup all-purpose flour
¼ cup tawny Port

For the spiced cream: In a saucepan, stir together the cream, onions, shallots, garlic, salt, peppercorns, nutmeg, and thyme. Bring the mixture to a boil over medium-high heat, then reduce heat to medium-low and simmer for about 20 minutes. Remove the saucepan from the heat and let stand, uncovered, for 1 hour. Cover with plastic and chill in the refrigerator overnight.

Strain the cream through a fine sieve, pressing on the solids to extract as much cream as possible. Measure the cream; there should be about 1½ cups. If there is more than 1½ cups of the cream, return it to the saucepan and simmer until reduced to 1½ cups. Set aside the spiced cream.

Preheat oven to 325 degrees. Line a 6-cup terrine mold or loaf pan with parchment paper and butter the parchment.

In a skillet, melt the butter over medium heat. Add the shallots and sauté until tender. With a rubber spatula, transfer the shallots and butter to the bowl of a food processor. Add the chilled pork, eggs, flour, and Port and process just until smooth. With the motor running, pour in the spiced cream and purée just until combined with the pork. Transfer the pork mixture to the prepared terrine and cover the terrine with the lid or foil. Place the terrine in a larger pan. Fill the pan with enough boiling water to come halfway up the sides of the terrine. Bake for about 1½ hours, or until a knife inserted in the center comes out clean. Uncover the terrine and let cool completely. Cover and chill in the refrigerator until cold. The boudin blanc can be made 3 days ahead. Unmold the boudin blanc onto a serving platter. Slice and serve with good bread.

Serves 10 to 12

MAY 9, 1805 — *we saved the best of the meat, and from the cow I killed we saved the necessary materials for making what our wrighthand cook Charbono calls the boudin (poudingue) blanc; and immediately set him about preparing them for supper; this white pudding we all esteem one of the greatest del[ic]acies of the forrest,* — LEWIS

Pork, Apples, and Prune Stew

In Virginia, pigs were allowed to run free and fatten themselves on roots, chestnuts, and whatever else they could find in the forests. They were then rounded up and slaughtered in the fall, providing fine hams, roasts, and sausages The apples and prunes in this savory stew are a sweet counterpoint to the flavor of the pork loin.

2½ pounds pork loin, cut into 1½-inch cubes
     Salt and freshly ground black pepper to taste
     All-purpose flour
¼ cup olive oil
1 leek, pale green part only, chopped
4 cups chicken stock
1 cup rice
3 tart cooking apples, peeled and thickly sliced
1 cup pitted prunes
1 tablespoon minced fresh sage

Preheat oven to 350 degrees.

Season the pork well with salt and pepper. Lightly dredge the pork in flour and shake off the excess. In a Dutch oven, heat the oil over medium-high heat. Add the pork and brown well on all sides. Add the leek and sauté until tender. Stir in the chicken stock, scraping up any browned bits. Bring the mixture to a simmer, then cover the pot, and cook in the oven for 1 hour.

Remove the pot from the oven and stir in the rice, apples, prunes, and sage. Cover the pot and return to the oven for 40 minutes, or until the pork is very tender. Remove from the oven and skim off any fat. Taste for seasoning and serve.

Serves 6

JUNE 25, 1804 — *The Praries come within a Short distance of the river on each Side which Contains in addition to Plumbs Raspberries &c. vast quantities of wild apples...* — CLARK

PLATE XII

SPERM WHALE

JANUARY 6, 1806 — *The last evening Shabono and his Indian woman was very impatient to be permitted to go with me, and was therefore indulged. She observed that She had traveled a long way with us to See the great waters, and that now that monstrous fish was also to be Seen, She thought it verry hard that She could not be permitted to See either (she had never yet been to the Ocian).* — CLARK

Sausage and White Bean Stew

During Jefferson's time 80 percent of a pig was used for food. What wasn't used as hams or bacon would find its way into various types of sausages and jellies. Together with a handful of beans and vegetables, a small quantity of sausage would make quite a remarkably good stew.

  2 cups white beans, soaked overnight in 6 cups water
1½ pounds bulk pork sausage
  3 cups chicken stock
1½ cups milk
  1 cup dry white wine
  1 onion, chopped
  2 carrots, chopped
  2 stalk celery, chopped
  2 cloves garlic, minced
  1 tablespoon minced fresh sage
  1 bay leaf
  1 teaspoon salt
 ½ teaspoon freshly ground black pepper

Preheat oven to 350 degrees.

Drain the white beans and discard the soaking liquid. Place the drained beans in a large pot. In a skillet over medium heat, brown the sausage. With a slotted spoon, transfer the sausage to the pot. Add the rest of the ingredients, cover the pot, and cook in the oven for 1 hour. Remove the lid and continue to cook for an additional 1 hour, or until the beans are tender and the liquid has been absorbed.

Serves 8

JANUARY 5, 1806 ⟶ . . . *the Indians were very friendly and had given them a considerable quantity of the blubber of a whale which perished on the coast some distance S E. of them; part of this blubber they brought with them, it was white & not unlike the fat of Poork, tho' the texture was more spongey and somewhat coarser. I had a part of it cooked and found it very pallitable and tender.* ⟶ LEWIS

Pork Braised in Milk and Fresh Herbs

To the early settlers, no other animal was as useful as the pig.
Capable of largely fending for itself, the farm hog provided bacon, sausage,
and ham. A treat available only during the fall was fresh pork roast,
which was often prepared in the following fashion.

¼ cup olive oil
2½ pounds pork tenderloin
1 tablespoon minced fresh oregano
1 tablespoon minced fresh rosemary
1 tablespoon minced fresh tarragon
2 teaspoons salt
1 teaspoon freshly ground black pepper
2¼ cups milk (approximately)

Preheat oven to 400 degrees. Oil a 3-quart Dutch oven.

Heat the olive oil in the Dutch oven over medium-high heat. Add the pork and brown well on all sides. Sprinkle with the oregano, rosemary, tarragon, salt, and pepper. Add enough milk to come halfway up the side of the pork. Cover the Dutch oven and cook in the oven for 1½ hours. Remove the lid and continue to cook until the milk forms a very thick sauce and the pork is golden brown.

Transfer the pork to a cutting board and let rest for 10 minutes before carving into ½-slices. Spoon the sauce over the roast and serve immediately.

Serves 6

APRIL 14, 1805 — *on these hills many aromatic herbs are seen; resembling in taste, smel and appearance, the sage, hysop, wormwood, southernwood, and two other herbs which are strangers to me;* — LEWIS

Maple Sugar-Glazed Smithfield Ham with Madeira-Raisin Sauce

Meriwether Lewis's mother, Lucy Marks, was known throughout Virginia for the quality of her Smithfield hams. Properly prepared, they have a piquant flavor reminiscent of the Virginia peanuts local pigs are raised on. After baking, slice the Smithfield ham in very thin slices and serve with the Madeira-Raisin Sauce.

1 Smithfield ham, about 14 pounds
1 cup maple sugar
2 teaspoons dry mustard
2 tablespoons water
2 cups Madeira
2 cups raisins
1 cup heavy cream
　Sweet Hot Mustard, page 22

Scrub the ham with a stiff brush. In a very large stockpot, soak the ham for 48 hours, changing the water every 8 hours.

Cover the ham in stockpot with fresh water and bring to a simmer over medium heat. Keep a candy thermometer clipped to the side of the pot to monitor the temperature of the water. The temperature should stay at 190 degrees. Simmer the ham for 25 minutes per pound. When the ham is cooked, transfer to a large cutting board. Cut off the skin and most of the fat underneath the skin and discard. Place the ham, fat-side up, in a large roasting pan.

Preheat oven to 350 degrees.

In a small bowl, stir together the maple sugar and dry mustard with a fork until blended. Add the water and stir until it forms a paste. Pat the paste over the top of the ham. Transfer the ham to the oven and bake for 1 hour.

Transfer the ham to a serving platter and tent with foil to keep warm. Place the roasting pan on the stovetop over two burners and turn the heat to medium.

Whisk in the Madeira, scraping up any browned bits. Simmer until the mixture has slightly thickened. Stir in the raisins and simmer until they plump. Whisk in the cream and simmer, whisking constantly, until the sauce has slightly thickened. Carve the ham at the table and pass the Madeira-Raisin Sauce and the Sweet Hot Mustard separately.

Serves 12

JUNE 1, 1801 — *We have at length heard from the person in Smithfield (Mr George Purdie) of whom enquiry was made some time ago respecting hams. Mr. P. is a person remarkable for curing good bacon* — GEORGE JEFFERSON to Jefferson

Braised Lamb Shanks with Rice

*Because most meals were prepared in open fireplaces, the Dutch oven
was an indispensable tool in early America.*

2	tablespoons olive oil
4	lamb shanks
2	cups dry white wine
1¾	cups tomato sauce
2	tablespoons freshly squeezed lemon juice
3	cloves garlic, minced
1½	teaspoons oregano
1	teaspoon salt
½	teaspoon freshly ground black pepper
¼	teaspoon dried hot chile flakes
1¼	cups rice

In a large Dutch oven, heat the olive oil over medium-high heat. Brown the lamb
shanks very well on all sides. Pour in the white wine and reduce the heat to
medium-low. Cover the Dutch oven and simmer for 1 hour. Add the tomato
sauce, lemon juice, garlic, oregano, salt, pepper, and chile flakes and stir to combine. Cover and continue simmering for 45 minutes. Skim off and discard the
excess fat. Stir in the rice, cover, and simmer about 30 minutes, or until the rice
is cooked.

Serves 4

JULY 29, 1806 — *on our way today we killed 9 bighorns...
the flesh of this animal is extreemly delicate tender
and well flavored, they are now in fine order.
their flesh both in colour and flavor much resembles mutton
though it is not so strong as our mutton.* — LEWIS

AUGUST 7, 1806 — We overtook the Fieldses at noon.
they had killed 2 bear and seen 6 others. we saw and fired on
two from our perogue but killed neither of them. these bears
resort to the river where they lie in water at the crossing
places of the game for Elk and weak cattle (buffaloe);
when they procure a subject of they lie by the carcase and
keep the wolves off until they devour it. the bear appear
to be very abundant on this part of the river. — LEWIS

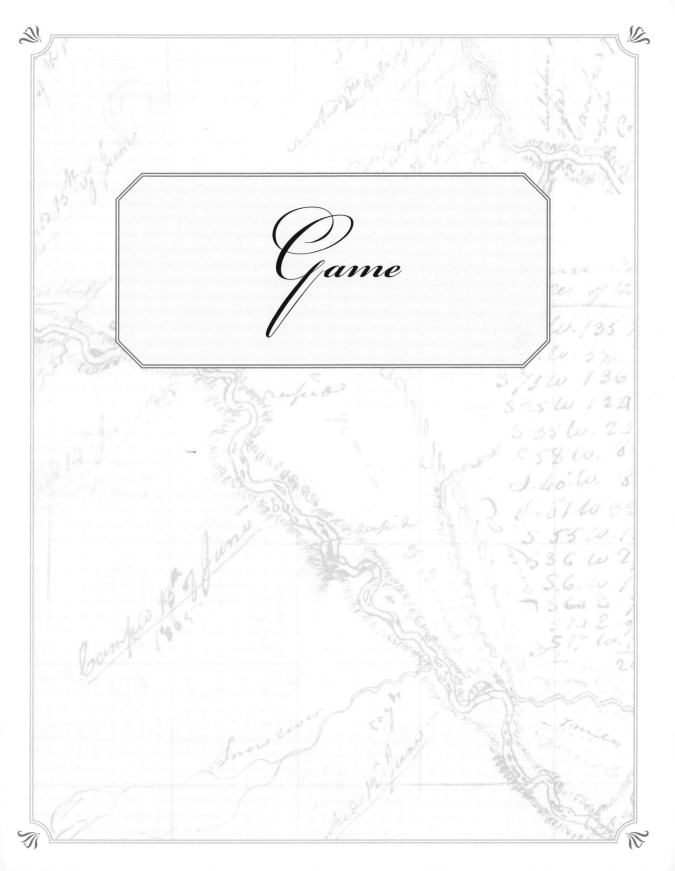

Game

Bear with Red Wine, Mushroom, and Juniper Sauce

Today we can special-order farm-raised bear that has a rich beefy flavor and a deep red color. During their trek across the continent, the Corps of Discovery at first did not believe the Native Americans' stories about the ferocity of the grizzly bear, also known as brown bears and silver bears. But a few close encounters changed their minds quickly.

Marinade:

- 4 cups red wine
- ¼ cup red wine vinegar
- 1 onion, chopped
- 1 carrot, chopped
- 3 cloves garlic, chopped
- 1½ teaspoons salt
- 20 dried juniper berries, minced
- ½ teaspoon whole black peppercorns
- 1 bay leaf

- 6- to 7-pound bear loin roast or beef sirloin roast
  Salt and freshly ground black pepper to taste
- 2 tablespoons butter
- 1 pound mushrooms, sliced

For the marinade: In a saucepan, combine the red wine, red wine vinegar, onion, carrot, garlic, salt, juniper berries, peppercorns, and bay leaf. Bring the mixture to a simmer over medium-high heat and continue to simmer for 3 minutes. Remove the saucepan from the heat and let stand until cool. Place the roast into a container just large enough to hold it. Pour the cooled marinade over the meat, cover with plastic wrap, and refrigerate overnight, turning the meat once.

Preheat oven to 325 degrees.

Place the roast in a roasting pan and season with salt and pepper. Set aside for 15 minutes.

Strain the marinade into a saucepan and discard the solids. Simmer the strained marinade over medium heat until the mixture is reduced to 1 cup. In a skillet, melt the butter over medium heat. Add the mushrooms and sauté until the mushrooms are tender and most of their liquid has evaporated. Add the mushrooms to the reduced marinade and keep warm.

Season the roast with salt and pepper. Insert a meat thermometer without touching the bone. Roast until the thermometer reaches 165 degrees. Remove the roast from the oven and let stand for 10 minutes before slicing. Serve with the sauce spooned over the sliced bear roast.

Serves 6 to 8

MAY 11, 1805 ⟶ About 5. P.M. my attention was struck by one of the Party running at a distance towards us and making signs and hollowing as if in distress, . . . he had shot a brown bear which immediately turned on him and pursued him a considerable distance . . . (we) shot him through the skull with two balls; we proceeded [to] dress him as soon as possible . . . it was a monstrous beast . . . I must confess that I do not like the gentlemen and had reather fight two Indians than one bear ⟶ LEWIS

GRIZZLY BEAR

Buffalo Stew with Suet Dumplings

The proper name for the American buffalo is the bison, since they are not related to the true buffalos of Asia and Africa. At one time, over 60 million bison roamed the prairies of America and supplied the Plains Indians with virtually all they needed, from bone needles to clothing. After being nearly exterminated by the end of the 19th century, the American bison has been brought back from the brink of extinction to today's population of over 200,000.

2 pounds buffalo or beef stew meat, cut into 1-inch cubes
Salt and freshly ground black pepper to taste
¼ cup all-purpose flour
2 tablespoons olive oil
½ cup brandy
2 tablespoons butter
½ cup finely chopped Smithfield ham or prosciutto
1 onion, finely chopped
2 carrots, sliced
2 teaspoons minced garlic
2 cups beef stock
2 cups dry red wine
2 tablespoons minced fresh parsley
1 bay leaf
½ teaspoon thyme

Suet Dumplings:
4 ounces suet
1½ cups all-purpose flour
½ teaspoon salt
½ cup cold water

Season the buffalo meat with salt and pepper and lightly toss together with the flour. In a large pot, heat the olive oil over medium-high heat. Add the buffalo and brown on all sides. Stir in the brandy, scraping up any browned bits, and simmer until almost all of the liquid has evaporated. Take care that the brandy does not flame up; if it does cover the pot with a lid to smother the flames. Transfer the buffalo to a bowl and set aside.

Add the butter to the pot and reduce the heat to medium. Add the ham and sauté until lightly browned. Add the onion and carrots and sauté until tender.

Add the garlic and sauté until fragrant. Return the buffalo and any accumulated juices to the pot. Stir in the beef stock, red wine, parsley, bay leaf, and thyme, and bring to a simmer. Cover the pot, reduce the heat to medium-low, and simmer for 2 hours, or until the buffalo is very tender.

For the suet dumplings: Place the suet in the bowl of a food processor and process until finely ground. Add the flour and salt and pulse until the mixture is well combined. With the motor running, pour in the water in a thin stream. Pulse until the dough comes together in a ball. Shape the dumplings into golf-ball sized balls.

Carefully add the dumplings to the simmering stew and turn them to coat in the sauce. Cover the pot and continue to cook an additional 25 minutes.

Serves 6

AMERICAN BISON

JUNE 26, 1805 — ... to myself I assign the duty of cook as well for those present as for the party which I expect again to arrive this evening from the lower camp. I collected my wood and water, boiled a large quantity of excellent dryed buffaloe meat and made each man a large suet dumpling by way of a treat. — LEWIS

Buffalo and Forest Mushroom
Shepherd's Pie

*Ideally suited to grazing on the native grasses of the great plains, a mature buffalo
or bison can weigh over 2500 pounds and stand over six feet at the shoulder.
Lower in cholesterol than beef, buffalo often sustained the members of the Corps of
Discovery during their long trek across the North American continent.*

Topping:
1½ pounds potatoes, peeled and quartered
¼ cup butter
¾ teaspoon salt

1 cup dried wild mushrooms, such as morels, chanterelles, or porcinis
1 cup beef stock
1 tablespoon olive oil
1 onion, finely chopped
1 carrot, finely diced
2 cloves garlic, minced
1 pound ground buffalo or ground beef
1 tablespoon all-purpose flour
¾ cup heavy cream
1 teaspoon salt
½ teaspoon freshly ground black pepper
½ teaspoon minced fresh rosemary
1 bay leaf
1 cup corn kernels

Preheat oven to 350 degrees. Lightly oil a 10-inch pie plate.

For the topping: In a pot, cover the potatoes with water. Cook the potatoes over
medium heat until tender. Drain the potatoes and mash them with the butter
and salt until smooth. Set aside.

In a small saucepan, combine the mushrooms and the beef stock. Bring to a simmer over medium heat. Remove from the heat, cover the saucepan, and let
stand for 30 minutes. With a slotted spoon, transfer the mushrooms to a cutting
board and finely chop. Set the mushrooms aside. Strain the mushroom soaking
liquid through a fine sieve lined with a double layer of moistened cheesecloth.
Set aside the strained liquid.

In a large skillet, heat the olive oil over medium heat. Add the onion and carrot and sauté until tender. Add the reserved mushrooms and garlic and sauté until most of the liquid has evaporated. Transfer the mushroom mixture to a bowl and set aside.

To the skillet, add the buffalo and sauté until browned and broken up. Return the mushroom mixture to the skillet and stir to mix. Stir in the reserved mushroom liquid and simmer until the liquid has almost evaporated. Sprinkle the flour over the buffalo mixture and stir until the flour is absorbed. Stir in the cream, salt, pepper, rosemary, and bay leaf and simmer until slightly thickened. Stir in the corn and transfer the mixture to the prepared pie plate. Spread the reserved mashed potatoes over the filling, sealing it to the edges. With the back of a spoon, make decorative swirls on the potatoes. Bake for about 25 minutes, or until the topping is golden brown.

Serves 6

AMERICAN BISON

APRIL 22, 1805 — *I assended to the top of the cutt bluff this morning, from whence I had a most delightful view of the country, the whole of which except the vally formed by the Missouri is void of timber or underbrush, exposing to the irst glance of the spectator immence herds of Buffaloe, Elk, deer, and Antelopes feeding in one common and boundless pasture.* — LEWIS

Honey and Beer-Braised Buffalo Ribs

*Braising the ribs, meat-side down, will make them tender and the
final roasting, meat-side up, will caramelize and crisp them.
Serve with soft polenta or mashed potatoes.*

6 to 7 pounds buffalo short ribs or beef short ribs
Salt and freshly ground black pepper to taste
¼ cup olive oil
3 onions, chopped
1 carrot, sliced
4 cloves garlic, minced
2 cups ale
½ cup chopped tomatoes
¼ cup honey
2 teaspoons Dijon mustard

Preheat oven to 350 degrees. Lightly oil a large roasting pan with a lid.

Season the ribs with salt and pepper. In a large skillet, heat the olive oil over medium-high heat. In batches, add the ribs, meat-side down, and brown well. Place the ribs meat-side down in the prepared roasting pan. Add the onions to the skillet and sauté until golden brown. Add the carrot and garlic and sauté until fragrant. Stir in the ale, tomatoes, honey, and mustard and bring to a simmer. Pour the onion mixture over the ribs. Cover the roasting pan and cook in the oven for 2 hours. Remove the lid and turn the ribs meat-side up. Return the roasting pan, uncovered, to the oven and cook an additional 30 minutes. Spoon the sauce over the ribs and serve immediately.

Serves 8

OCTOBER 21 1805 — *One of our party J. Collins presented us
with Some verry good beer made of the Pa-shi-co-quar-mash
bread, which bread is the remains of what was laid in as a part
of our Stores and Provisions.* — CLARK

PLATE XIII

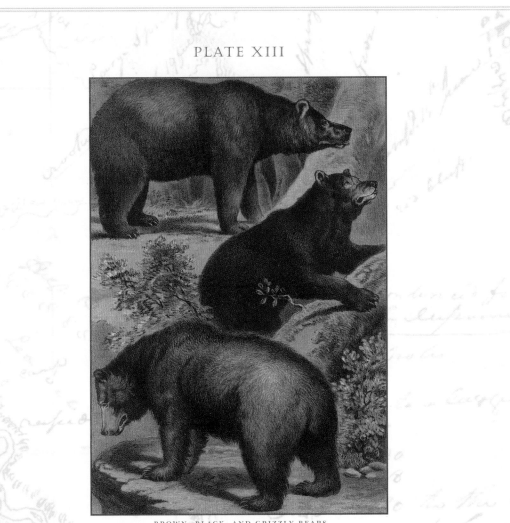

BROWN, BLACK, AND GRIZZLY BEARS

JULY 15, 1806 — ... McNeal returned with his musquet broken off at the breach and informed me that... he had approached a white bear within ten feet without discover[ing] him the bear being in the thick brush, the horse took the allarm and turning short threw him... under the bear; this animal raised himself on his hinder feet for battle, and gave him time to recover from his fall... and with his clubbed musquet he struck the bear over the head and cut him, the bear stunned... fell to the ground; ... this gave McNeal time to climb a willow tree... and thus made his escape. — LEWIS

Buffalo Liver with Madeira Sauce

*Originally from a Portuguese colony off the northern coast of Africa
Madeira is a sweet wine that was extremely popular in the
17th and 18th centuries both in Europe and America.
Used to deglaze the pan, the Madeira imparts a sublime sweet richness to the liver.
A whole buffalo liver can weigh more than twelve pounds, so order only
the amount you need for this recipe.*

  2 pounds buffalo liver or veal liver
      Milk
      Salt and freshly ground black pepper to taste
      All-purpose flour for dredging
  ¼ cup butter
  ½ cup finely chopped onion
  1½ cups Madeira
  ½ cup sour cream

Cut the liver into 1½-inch thick by 5-inch long strips. Place the strips in a large bowl and completely cover with milk. Cover the bowl and refrigerate overnight.

Remove the liver from the milk and pat dry. Season the liver with salt and pepper and dredge in the flour. In a large skillet, melt the butter over medium heat. Add the liver in batches and brown on all sides. Remove the browned liver pieces to a shallow dish. Add the onion to the skillet and sauté until tender. Whisk in the Madeira, scraping up any browned bits. Whisk in the sour cream until smooth. Return the liver and any accumulated juices to the skillet, and simmer until the liver is completely cooked and the sauce has thickened.

Serves 8

MAY 9, 1805 — we saw a great quantity of game today particularly of Elk and Buffaloe, the latter are now so gentle that the men frequently throw sticks and stones at them in order to drive them out of the way. — LEWIS

Glazed Buffalo Meatloaf

As Lewis and Clark discovered, buffalo meat has a rich beefy taste and can be substituted for beef in most recipes. The choicest cuts are the sirloin roast and the rump roast. For this meatloaf recipe, ground buffalo is used, which is somewhat leaner than standard ground hamburger.

Meatloaf:
   3 tablespoons butter
   1 onion, finely chopped
   1 stalk celery, finely chopped
   ½ teaspoon dried thyme
   2 eggs, beaten
   ½ cup oatmeal
   ⅓ cup Tomato Catsup, see page 23, or ketchup
   2 teaspoons salt
   1 teaspoon freshly ground black pepper
   2 pounds ground buffalo or ground beef

Glaze:
   ½ cup Tomato Catsup, see page 23, or ketchup
   ⅓ cup packed brown sugar
   2 teaspoons dry mustard
   ¼ teaspoon ground nutmeg

Preheat oven to 350 degrees. Lightly oil a 9 by 9-inch baking dish.

For the meatloaf: In a skillet, melt the butter over medium heat. Add the onion, celery, and thyme and sauté until tender. Remove the skillet from the heat and set aside to cool.

In a large bowl, whisk together the eggs, oatmeal, catsup, salt, and pepper. Stir in the cooled onion mixture. Add the ground buffalo and mix with your hands until well combined with no lumps. Transfer the mixture to the prepared baking dish, smoothing the top.

For the glaze: In a small bowl, whisk together the catsup, brown sugar, mustard, and nutmeg until smooth. Spread the glaze evenly over the top of the meatloaf. Bake for about 1 hour, or until a meat thermometer inserted in the center of the meatloaf reads 145 degrees. Let the meatloaf rest for 10 minutes before serving.

Serves 8

AUGUST 23, 1804 — *We stopped at a prairie on the north side, the largest and handsomest, which I had seen. Captain Clarke called it Buffaloe prairie. The men having returned, we again went on; but the wind changed and we were obliged to halt for the present. While we were detained here we salted two barrels of buffaloe meat.* — GASS

AMERICAN BISON

Herbed Buffalo Tongue with Shallot and Horseradish Sauce

Tender with a mild flavor, the tongue was the most prized part of the buffalo and can be prepared in the same fashion as beef tongue. Excellent when prepared as follows, it is also delicious when eaten simply in a sandwich with fresh horseradish spread.

2 to 3 pound buffalo tongue or beef tongue
1 onion, quartered
1 carrot, sliced
1 stalk celery, sliced
1 leek, pale green part only, sliced
2 tablespoons chopped fresh parsley
2 tablespoons cider vinegar
2 cloves garlic, bruised
1 teaspoon dried thyme
½ teaspoon dried sage
½ teaspoon salt
6 whole black peppercorns

Shallot and Horseradish Sauce:
¼ cup butter
½ cup finely chopped shallots
¾ cup sour cream
¼ cup heavy cream
2 tablespoons prepared horseradish
1 tablespoon freshly squeezed lemon juice
1 tablespoon grainy mustard
   Salt and freshly ground black pepper to taste
¼ cup minced fresh parsley

In a pot, combine the tongue, onion, carrot, celery, leek, parsley, vinegar, garlic, thyme, sage, salt, and peppercorns. Add enough boiling water to cover the tongue. Bring to a simmer over medium-high heat, then reduce heat to medium-low. Simmer, uncovered, for about 3 hours, or until very tender. Add more boiling water to the pot as needed.

For the sauce: In a saucepan, melt the butter over medium heat. Add the shallots and sauté until tender. Stir in the sour cream, cream, horseradish, lemon juice, mustard, salt, and pepper and bring to a simmer over medium heat. Reduce heat to medium-low and simmer until the mixture has thickened to a sauce consistency. Stir in the parsley and heat through.

Remove the tongue from the pot and let cool enough to handle. Remove and discard the skin and trim off any gristle. Slice slightly on the diagonal and serve with the sauce.

Serves 6 to 8

AMERICAN BISON

JUNE 13, 1805 — *My fare is really sumptuous this evening; buffaloe's humps, tongues and marrowbones; fine trout parched meal pepper and salt, and a good appetite; the last is not considered the least of the luxuries.* — LEWIS

Rack of Venison with a Rosemary-Dijon Crust

Derived from the Latin word venari, which means "to hunt," venison actually refers to the meat of all large game animals with antlers, including elk and antelope, but most commonly refers to deer meat. Farm-raised venison does not have the intense game flavor of the wild version—excellent for those who prefer milder flavored meat. Have your meat cutter French the rack and plan to serve at least two rib sections per guest. If you desire, cover the rib tips with aluminum foil to prevent them from burning during roasting.

Rosemary Dijon-Crust:
- ½ cup olive oil
- 2 tablespoons Dijon mustard
- 2 teaspoons finely minced fresh rosemary
- 3 cloves garlic, minced
- 1 teaspoon salt
- ½ teaspoon freshly ground black pepper
- 1 cup dry bread crumbs

- 1 rack (about 2 pounds) of venison or 2 racks of lamb
  Salt and freshly ground black pepper to taste
- 2 tablespoons olive oil

Preheat oven to 375 degrees. Lightly oil a roasting pan.

For the crust: In a small bowl, stir together the olive oil, Dijon, rosemary, garlic, salt, and pepper. Add the bread crumbs and stir until blended. Set aside.

Season the rack of venison with salt and pepper. In a skillet, heat the 2 tablespoons of olive oil over medium-high heat. When hot, sear the venison on both sides. Place the venison fat-side up in the prepared roasting pan. Press the crust mixture over the fat-side of the rack. Roast until a meat thermometer reads 136 degrees. Remove from the oven and let rest 5 minutes before carving.

Serves 4 to 6

JUNE 7, 1805 — during the day we had killed six deer some of them in very good order altho' none of them had yet entirely discarded their winter coats. We had reserved and brought with us a good supply of the best pieces; we roasted and eat a hearty supper of our venison not having taisted a mo[r]sel before during the day; I now laid myself down on some willow boughs to a comfortable nights rest, and felt indeed as if I was fully repaid for the toil and pain of the day, so much will a good shelter, a dry bed, and comfortable supper revive the sperits of the w[e]aryed, wet and hungry traveler. — LEWIS

WHITE-TAIL DEER

Grilled Venison Chops with Red Wine Sauce

Throughout their travels, the Corps of Discovery relied upon their success at hunting deer to provide sufficient food. Each man ate an average of 9 pounds of meat per day — that is, when they could get it!

¼ cup olive oil
1 tablespoon minced garlic
1 teaspoon salt
½ teaspoon freshly ground black pepper
8 venison rib chops

1 tablespoon minced fresh parsley

Red Wine Sauce:

1 tablespoon butter
2 shallots, minced
1 tablespoon red wine vinegar
¾ cup red wine
¾ cup beef stock
2 tablespoons red currant jelly
Salt and freshly ground black pepper to taste

In a small bowl, stir together the olive oil, garlic, salt, and pepper. Rub this mixture all over the venison chops. Cover the chops and refrigerate for 3 hours.

For the red wine sauce: In a saucepan, melt the butter over medium heat. Add the shallots and sauté until tender. Whisk in the vinegar and sauté until the liquid has almost evaporated. Stir in the red wine and simmer until the liquid has reduced by half. Stir in the beef stock and simmer until the liquid has reduced by half. Whisk in the jelly, salt, and pepper and heat through.

Prepare a hot grill. Grill the venison chops for about 2 minutes per side, or until medium-rare. Do not overcook. Serve with the sauce spooned over the chops and sprinkled with the parsley.

Serves 4

JULY 4, 1806 — *This being the day of the decleration of Independence of the United States and a Day commonly scelebrated by my Country I had every disposition to selebrate this day and therefore halted early and partook of a Sumptious Dinner of a fat Saddle of Venison and Mush of Cows (roots)* — CLARK

PLATE XIV

MOOSE, DEER, AND ELK

AUGUST 1, 1806 ⁓ *The Elk are now in fine order particularly the males. Their horns have obtained their full growth, but not yet shed the velvet or skin which covers them.* ⁓ CLARK

Venison Shanks Braised with Fennel and Onions

Slow-cooked for more than two hours, with a highly savory and delicious sauce, these lean and healthy venison shanks are one of the most delicious cuts of meat. This requires a very large Dutch oven, available through Lodge Cast Iron. See Resources on page 151.

3 tablespoons olive oil	½ teaspoon dried basil
6 venison shanks or lamb shanks	½ teaspoon dried marjoram
Salt and freshly ground	½ teaspoon dried oregano
black pepper to taste	½ teaspoon dried rosemary
¾ cup dry red wine	½ teaspoon dried sage
3 cups beef stock	½ teaspoon dried thyme
⅔ cup red currant jelly	2 bulbs fennel, quartered
1 tablespoon red wine vinegar	1 onion, quartered
3 cloves garlic, minced	2 carrots, sliced

In a very large Dutch oven, heat the olive oil over medium-high heat. Season the venison with salt and pepper. Brown the venison shanks very well on all sides. Arrange them in a single layer in the Dutch oven. Add the wine, scraping up any browned bits. Add the beef stock, currant jelly, vinegar, garlic, basil, marjoram, oregano, rosemary, sage, and thyme and reduce the heat to medium-low. Cover the Dutch oven and simmer for 1½ hours. Add the fennel, onion, and carrots. Cover and continue simmering for 45 minutes, or until the venison and vegetables are very tender.

Remove the venison and vegetables to a large serving bowl and tent with foil to keep warm. Increase the heat to medium-high under the Dutch oven and simmer the sauce until it has reduced to a sauce consistency. Skim off any fat. Pour the sauce over the venison and vegetables and serve.

Serves 6

MAY 16, 1806 — *Shabono's [wife] gathered a quantity of fenel roots which we find a very paliatiable and nurushing food. the onion we also find in abundance and boil it with our meat.* — CLARK

Venison Roulade Stuffed with Mushrooms and Smithfield Ham

Most venison tastes best when simmered or braised in a savory broth. Here the combination of Smithfield ham and wild mushrooms lends a complex and fragrant aroma and flavor to the delicate and tender rolled venison steak.

Filling:
- 1 cup dried wild mushrooms such as morels, chanterelles, or porcini
- 1½ cups boiling water
- ½ cup minced Smithfield ham or prosciutto
- ¼ cup dried bread crumbs
- 2 egg yolks
- 1 tablespoon finely minced onion
- ½ teaspoon salt
- ¼ teaspoon freshly ground black pepper

- 1½ pounds venison round steak or beef flank steak
  Salt and freshly ground black pepper to taste
  All-purpose flour
- 3 tablespoons olive oil
- 1 cup dry red wine

- 2 tablespoons all-purpose flour
- 1 tablespoon butter, softened

- 1 pound rotini or other spiral pasta, cooked in
  boiling salted water until al dente, then drained

For the filling: Place the dried mushrooms in a bowl. Pour the boiling water over the mushrooms and let stand until cool. With a slotted spoon, transfer the mushrooms to a cutting board. Strain the mushroom soaking liquid through a fine sieve lined with a double layer of moistened cheesecloth. Set aside the strained mushroom liquid.

Finely chop the mushrooms and mix with the ham, bread crumbs, egg yolks, onion, salt, and pepper. Stir to combine.

Remove the bone from the round steak and pound the steak with a meat mallet on both sides until it is uniformly ½-inch thick. Season with salt and pepper.

Spread the filling evenly over the meat. Roll up, jelly-roll fashion, and secure with kitchen string or toothpicks. Dust the roulade on all sides with the flour, brushing off the excess.

In a straight-sided skillet, heat the olive oil over medium-high heat. Add the roulade and brown well on all sides. Pour in the reserved mushroom liquid and red wine. Bring to a simmer, then reduce heat to medium-low, cover skillet, and simmer for about 1½ hours. Turn the roulade once during cooking.

Remove the roulade to a cutting board and let rest 10 minutes before slicing. In a small bowl blend together the 2 tablespoons of flour with the butter until smooth. Whisk the mixture into the sauce in the skillet. Increase the heat under the skillet to medium and continue to whisk until the sauce has thickened slightly. Divide the pasta among 6 plates. Slice the roulade into 1-inch slices and divide onto the pasta. Spoon the sauce over the meat and serve immediately.

Serves 6

PRONGHORN ANTELOPE

AUGUST 23, 1805 — the Indians pursued a mule buck near our camp I saw this chase for about 4 miles it was really entertaining, there were about twelve of them in pursuit of it on horseback, they finally rode it down and killed it. — LEWIS

Elk Roast with Orange, Cranberry, and Bourbon Sauce

Mentioned by travelers throughout the early history of North America, cranberries were one of the treasures of the fall berry harvest. Native to boggy areas where elk were also found, the sweet-sour cranberries provide a delicious counterpoint to the dark meat flavor of the roast.

2 cups cranberries	1 teaspoon salt
1 cup orange juice	½ teaspoon freshly ground
½ cup packed brown sugar	black pepper
½ cup finely chopped onion	3 pounds elk roast or
⅓ cup Kentucky bourbon	beef rump roast
1 tablespoon minced garlic	6 slices bacon

In a bowl large enough to hold the elk roast, stir together the cranberries, orange juice, brown sugar, onion, bourbon, garlic, salt, and pepper. Place the elk in the marinade, cover, and refrigerate overnight, turning once.

Preheat oven to 350 degrees.

Transfer the elk to a roasting pan and pour the marinade into a saucepan. Lay the strips of bacon over the elk and roast until a meat thermometer reads 136 degrees.

Bring the marinade to a boil over medium heat. Reduce the heat to medium-low and simmer until the sauce is very thick, stirring often to prevent scorching. Transfer the cranberry sauce to a serving dish. Transfer the elk to a cutting board and let rest for 10 minutes before slicing. Discard the bacon. Serve with the cranberry sauce on the side.

Serves 8

DECEMBER 8, 1805 — *I prosue'd this gang of Elk through bogs which the wate of a man would Shake for ½ an Acre, and maney places I Sunk into the Mud and water up to my hips without finding any bottom on the trale of those Elk. Those bogs are covered with a kind of Moss among which I observe an abundance of Cranberries.* — CLARK

Rabbit Smothered with Onions in Mustard Sauce

Rabbits were numerous and often enjoyed by the Corps of Discovery when no other game was available. Excellent when served with Homemade Noodles, page 15.

¼ cup butter
2 onions, coarsely chopped
1 rabbit (about 3 pounds) cut into serving pieces
   Salt and freshly ground black pepper to taste
   All-purpose flour
2 cups dry white wine
½ cup sour cream
3 tablespoons grainy mustard

In a large skillet, melt the butter over medium heat. Add the onions and sauté until golden brown. Remove the onions with a slotted spoon and set aside.

Season the rabbit pieces with salt and pepper. Dredge lightly in flour and shake off the excess. Add the rabbit to the skillet and brown well on all sides. Stir in the wine, scraping up any browned bits. Add the reserved onions. Cover the skillet, reduce heat to medium-low, and simmer for 30 minutes. Remove the lid and continue to simmer for an additional 30 minutes, or until the liquid has reduced to about ½ cup. Stir in the sour cream and mustard and simmer until thick and bubbly. Serve over pasta.

Serves 4 to 6

RABBIT

APRIL 12, 1805 — *Several of the hunters went out hunting. Capt Clark went out a short distance and killed [a] white rabit. found wild Onions &. C.* — ORDWAY

PUMPKIN

SEPTEMBER 5, 1806 — *the report of the guns which was heard must have been the Mahars who most probably have just arrived at their village to secure their crops of corn Beens punkins &c &c.* — CLARK

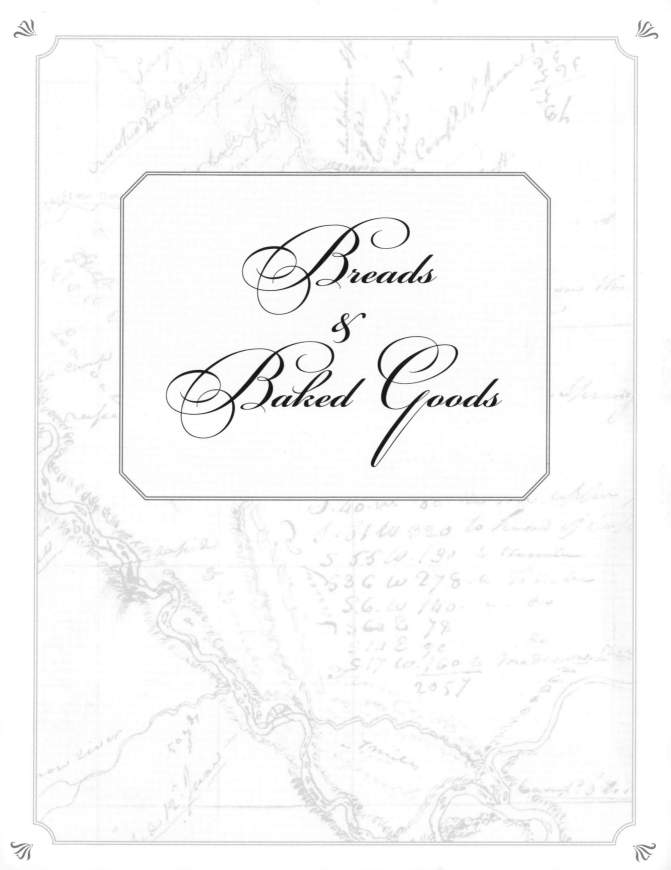

Breads
&
Baked Goods

Buttermilk Biscuits

*Biscuits were a staple of pioneers because they were easy to make,
filling, and delicious. Enjoy them on the trail out of a cast-iron Dutch
oven or off the baking sheet at home on a Sunday morning.*

1¾   cups all-purpose flour
2   teaspoons baking powder
1   teaspoon sugar
½   teaspoon salt
¼   cup cold butter, cut into small pieces
¾   cup buttermilk

Preheat oven to 450 degrees.

In a bowl, stir together the flour, baking powder, sugar, and salt with a fork until blended. Cut in the butter until the mixture resembles coarse meal. Stir in the buttermilk until the dough comes together. Turn out the dough onto a lightly floured board and pat out 1-inch thick. Cut out biscuits with a 2½-inch cookie cutter. Transfer the biscuits to a baking sheet. Bake for about 10 minutes, or until lightly golden brown.

Makes 8 biscuits

NOVEMBER 30, 1805 — [Sacagawea] gave me a piece of bread made of flour which She had reserved for her child and carefully Kept untill this time, which has unfortunately got wet, and a little Sour This bread I eate with great satisfaction, it being the only mouthfull I had tasted for Several months past. — CLARK

Cornbread

*Long cultivated by Native Americans and readily adopted by early settlers
and frontiersmen, corn was an indispensable staple in the New World.
Native American corn was grown in a staggering variety of colors and sizes.*

½ cup sugar
⅓ cup butter, softened
2 eggs
1 cup buttermilk
1 teaspoon baking soda
¾ cup cornmeal
2 teaspoons baking powder
1 teaspoon salt
1 cup all-purpose flour

Preheat oven to 350 degrees. Lightly oil a 9 by 9-inch pan.

In a bowl, cream together the sugar and butter until smooth. Add the eggs one
at a time, beating well after each addition. Dissolve the baking soda in the buttermilk and stir into the creamed mixture. In a separate bowl, combine the cornmeal, baking powder, and salt. Add to the creamed mixture and stir until well
blended. Add the flour and stir well. Pour into the prepared pan. Bake for about
20 minutes, or until a toothpick inserted in the center comes out clean.

JULY 6, 1808 — *I reserved very few of Gov⁻. Lewis's
articles, and have growing only his salsafia,
Mandane corn, and a pea remarkable for it's
beautiful blossom & leaf.* — JEFFERSON

Hushpuppies

*Legend has it that fishermen and hunters kept their dogs quiet by tossing them
little scraps of batter fried in the lard leftover from frying their catfish.
Soon the "Hushpuppies" became a favorite, and have been a Southern tradition
ever since. Serve them with the Cornmeal Crusted Catfish on page 43
and enjoy the flavor of the lower Mississippi River States.*

1½ cups cornmeal
1 teaspoon salt
1 teaspoon sugar
¼ teaspoon baking soda
2 eggs
½ cup buttermilk
¼ cup minced chives
Oil for frying

In a bowl, stir together the cornmeal, salt, sugar, and baking soda with a fork until
blended. Whisk in the eggs and buttermilk until smooth. Stir in the chives. In a
skillet, heat 1 inch of oil over medium-high heat. Drop the hushpuppy batter by
the tablespoonfuls into the hot oil. Cook until browned on both sides. Drain on
paper towels and serve hot.

Serves 6

OCTOBER 30, 1804 — *the natives were a number of the men &
women about our camp [who came] with Some corn and
Bread made of the corn meal parched & mixed with fat & C.
which eats verry well, they expect us to give them Some Small
article in return for their produce, Such as corn Beans
Squasshes & C of which they raise pleanty off for themselves
& to trade with other nations* — ORDWAY

PLATE XV

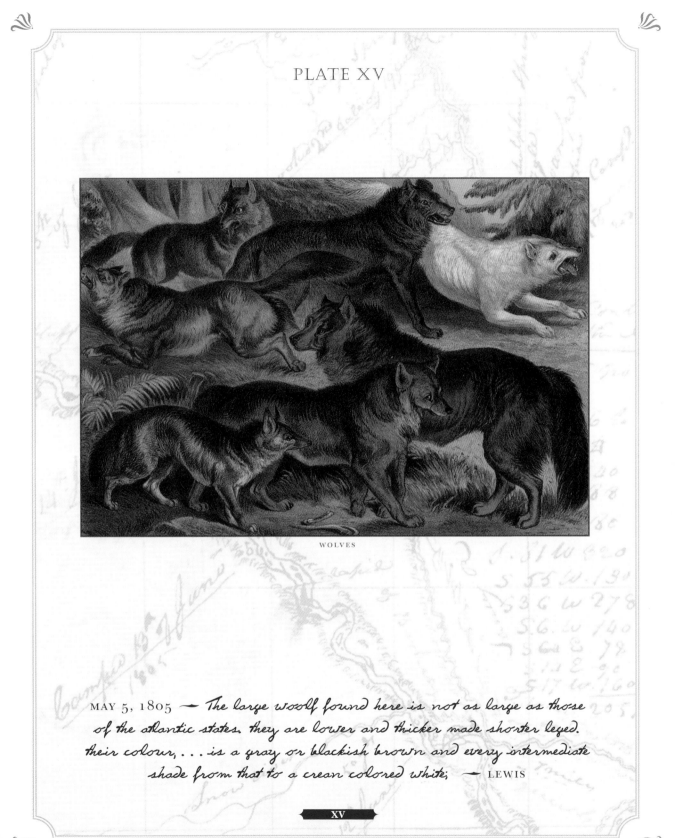

WOLVES

MAY 5, 1805 — The large woolf found here is not as large as those of the atlantic states. they are lower and thicker made shorter leged. their colour, . . . is a gray or blackish brown and every intermediate shade from that to a crean colored white; — LEWIS

Spoon Bread with Corn and Chives

Spoon bread is the thoroughly American variation on polenta. Commonly served during the time of our founding fathers and popular at every level of society, spoon bread is yet one more example of the rich culinary legacy that occurred from the fusion of Native American ingredients with European traditions.

3 cups milk	⅛ teaspoon cayenne
⅓ cup butter	1 cup cornmeal
2 teaspoons sugar	3 eggs, beaten
1½ teaspoons salt	1 cup corn kernels
½ teaspoon ground white pepper	1 tablespoon minced fresh chives

Preheat oven to 350 degrees. Lightly oil a 2-quart baking dish.

In a saucepan, stir together the milk, butter, sugar, salt, white pepper, and cayenne. Bring the mixture to a boil over medium-high heat. Slowly add the cornmeal a little at a time, whisking constantly, until the mixture thickens. Remove the saucepan from the heat and whisk in the beaten eggs. Stir in the corn and chives. Transfer the mixture to the prepared baking dish. Bake for about 35 to 40 minutes, or until the center is barely set. Serve warm.

Serves 6

CHIVES

MARCH 29, 1806 — observed a speceies of small wild onion growing among the moss on the rocks, they resemble the shives of our gardens and grow remarkably close together forming a perfect turf, they are as quite as agreeably flavoured as the shives. — LEWIS

Pumpkin Pecan Bread

This delectable sweet bread combines two quintessentially American ingredients, pumpkins and pecans. Native to North America, squash and particularly the pumpkin, were immediately embraced by the early settlers. There are records of the Connecticut field pumpkin being cultivated since 1700 and the small sugar pumpkin since the Civil War. Both varieties are the most commonly cultivated to this day.

1 cup pumpkin purée	1 teaspoon baking soda
½ cup vegetable oil	1 teaspoon ground cinnamon
½ cup water	¾ teaspoon salt
2 eggs	½ teaspoon ground allspice
1 cup sugar	½ teaspoon ground cloves
½ cup packed brown sugar	¼ teaspoon baking powder
1⅔ cups all-purpose flour	½ cup chopped pecans

Preheat oven to 325 degrees. Butter and flour a 9 by 5-inch loaf pan.

In a large bowl combine the pumpkin purée, oil, water, and eggs and beat until smooth. Add the sugar and brown sugar and beat until smooth. In a separate bowl, sift together the flour, baking soda, cinnamon, salt, allspice, cloves, and baking powder. Add to the pumpkin mixture and beat until smooth. Stir in the pecans. Pour the batter into the prepared loaf pan. Bake for about 1 hour and 15 minutes, or until a toothpick inserted in the center comes out clean. Let the pumpkin bread cool for 5 minutes in the pan before turning out on a rack to cool completely.

Makes 1 loaf

OCTOBER 10, 1804 — *I went down to the village which was built on the Island. found their lodges in this village about 60 in nomber and verry close compact. in a round form large & warm[ly] covered first after the wood is willows and Grass. Then a thick coat of Earth &. C. except the chimney hole which Goes out at center & top. they Raise considerable of Indian corn, beans pumkins Squasshes water millons a kind of Tobaco &. C.* — ORDWAY

Gingerbread

Ginger was a rare and expensive spice imported from Asia, and was used
only on special occasions, hence its association with holidays.
This recipe yields a thick, dense, and dark gingerbread—not to be confused
with the ginger cookie used to make gingerbread men and gingerbread houses.
This recipe is better the day after baking, becoming moister and more flavorful.
Serve with a dollop of sweetened whipped cream.

½ cup butter, softened
½ cup sugar
1 egg
1 cup molasses
1 cup boiling water
2½ cups all-purpose flour
1½ teaspoons baking soda
1 teaspoon ground cinnamon
1 teaspoon ground ginger
½ teaspoon salt
¼ teaspoon ground cloves

Preheat oven to 350 degrees. Lightly oil a 9 by 9-inch baking pan.

In a large bowl, cream together the butter and sugar. Add the egg and beat until fluffy. In a small bowl, stir together the molasses and boiling water until blended. In a separate bowl sift together the flour, baking soda, cinnamon, ginger, salt, and cloves. Add the flour mixture to the creamed mixture alternately with the molasses mixture, beating well after each addition. Pour the batter into the prepared pan and bake for 40 to 45 minutes, or until a toothpick inserted in the center comes out clean.

Serves 12

OCTOBER 21, 1805 — *bought some pounded fish from the Natives and some roots bread which was made up in cakes in form of ginger bread and eat verry well.* — WHITEHOUSE

Sweet Potato and Pecan Muffins

While Ambassador to France, Thomas Jefferson wrote to his relatives at home in Virginia requesting that sweet potato seeds be sent to him. Jefferson maintained a large garden in Paris where he cultivated North American fruits and vegetables which he introduced to the European court. These muffins, brimming with grated sweet potatoes and nuts are rich, moist, and incredibly flavorful. Excellent with sliced melons for a late summer brunch.

⅔ cup sugar
⅓ cup butter, softened
1 egg
1 teaspoon vanilla extract
1¾ cups all-purpose flour
1½ teaspoons baking powder
½ teaspoon salt
⅔ cup milk
1½ cups lightly packed, finely grated sweet potato
½ cup chopped pecans

Preheat oven to 375 degrees. Lightly oil a 12-cup muffin pan.

In a large bowl, cream together the sugar and butter until light and fluffy. Beat in the egg and vanilla until smooth. In a bowl, blend the flour, baking powder, and salt together with a fork. Add the flour mixture to the sugar mixture alternately with milk, beating until just combined. Fold in the sweet potato and pecans.

Pour the batter into the muffin cups almost filling them. Bake for about 25 minutes, or until a toothpick inserted in the center comes out clean. Serve warm.

Makes about 12 muffins

APRIL 30, 1806 — *This plain as usial is covered with arromatic shrubs, herbatious plants and tufts of short grass. maney of those plants produce those esculent roots which form a principal part of the subsistence of the natives. among others there is one which produces a root somewhat like the sweet potato.* — CLARK

PLATE XVI

PEACH

APRIL 13, 1804 ❧ *The peach trees are partly in blume the brant, Geese, Duck, Swan, Crain and other aquatic birds have disappeared verry much, within a few days and have gorn further North I prosume...* ❧ LEWIS

XVI

Cornmeal and Blueberry Mush

Cooked mixtures of cornmeal and native berries were a staple for the early explorers and colonists. The blueberry is a hardy New England native that flourishes in cold climates and rocky soils. It was one of the first fruits to be cultivated and hybridized in North America.

1½ cups milk
1½ cups water
½ teaspoon salt
¾ cup cornmeal
2 cups fresh blueberries
¼ cup maple syrup or honey

In a saucepan, stir together the milk, water, and salt. Bring the mixture to a boil over medium-high heat. Whisking constantly, slowly add the cornmeal a little at a time. Reduce the heat to medium and continue whisking until the mixture has slightly thickened. Remove the saucepan from the heat and stir in the blueberries and maple syrup. Divide into 6 bowls and serve.

Serves 6

DECEMBER 23, 1804 — a fine Day great numbers of indians of all discriptions Came to the fort many of them bringing Corn to trade, the little Crow, loadᵈ his wife & Sun with Corn for us, Cap. Lewis gave him a few presents as also his wife, She made a kittle of boiled Cimnins, beens, Corn & Choke Cheries with the Stones, which was palitable This Desh is Considered, as a treat among those people, — CLARK

Belgian Waffles with Maple Syrup

*Thomas Jefferson was intrigued by the Belgian tradition of pouring a liquid batter
onto a hot griddle. While in Flanders he purchased a waffle iron for
1.3 florins to take back to the kitchens at Monticello.
The widespread production of maple syrup and maple sugar began in the
American colonies in the early 17th century. The sap was tapped from maple trees
then boiled down to create syrup. Removing all the water from the sap produced
maple sugar. Somewhat less sweet than cane sugar, maple sugar imparts
a rich flavor to baked goods.*

  2 cups milk, warmed
 ½ cup melted butter
1½ teaspoons dry yeast
  2 cups all-purpose flour
  2 tablespoons sugar
  1 teaspoon salt
  3 eggs

  Maple syrup as an accompaniment

In a large bowl, stir together the milk, butter, and yeast and let stand for 5 minutes. Whisk in the flour, sugar, and salt until smooth. Cover with plastic wrap and let stand at room temperature overnight.

Preheat a waffle iron. Just before making the waffles, add the eggs to the batter and whisk until smooth. Pour about ½ cup of the batter into the hot waffle iron and cook until golden brown and crisp. Serve immediately with maple syrup.

Makes about 12 waffles

MAY 1, 1791 — *I shall be glad to hear how the white wheat,
mountain rice, Paccan & Sugar Maples have succeeded.
Evidence grows upon us that the U. S. may not only
supply themselves sugar for their own consumption
but be great exporters.* — JEFFERSON to Thomas Mann Randolph

A Quire of Paper Pancakes

*A "quire" is a set of 24 sheets of paper, and these exquisitely thin crepes may be
filled, rolled, or folded as easily as paper. This is how Mary Randolph,
a relative of Thomas Jefferson, described her famously paper-thin crepes
in her cookbook* The Virginia Housekeeper.

¾ cup all-purpose flour
1 cup milk, divided
2 eggs
2 tablespoons butter, melted and cooled
2 tablespoons sugar
⅛ teaspoon salt

    Additional melted butter for cooking the crepes

Sift the flour into a large bowl and make a well in the center. Place ½ cup of the
milk, the eggs, butter, sugar, and salt into the well. Starting from the center,
whisk ingredients together until smooth. Pour in the remaining ½ cup milk and
whisk vigorously until the batter is smooth. Cover and refrigerate the batter for
at least 1 hour, or overnight, before cooking the crepes.

Heat an 8-inch crepe pan over medium-high heat. Lightly brush with melted
butter. Pour in about 3 tablespoons of the batter and tilt the pan in all directions
to coat the bottom evenly. Cook until the top looks dry and brown spots appear
on the bottom, about 2 minutes. With a spatula, flip the crepe and cook for a few
more seconds until just golden. Remove the crepe to a plate and cover with a
kitchen towel to keep warm. Repeat with remaining batter and stack the finished
crepes on the plate.

Makes about 12 crepes

AUGUST 4, 1793 — *I inclose you two of Petit's recipes.
The orthography will amuse you: the word pancakes —
the French cook spelling it thus: pannequaiques.*

— JEFFERSON to Martha Jefferson Randolph

Buttermilk Huckleberry Pancakes

Huckleberries grow wild in the mountainous regions of the Pacific Northwest,
areas explored by the Corps of Discovery as they traveled down the Columbia River,
but because they are rather tart and very seedy, they are seldom grown commercially.
Enjoy these light and airy griddlecakes with a pot of warm maple syrup,
a cup of hot coffee and a couple of rashers of applewood-smoked bacon. If you don't
live where you can easily gather huckleberries, blueberries are just as good.

1⅔ cups buttermilk
1 teaspoon baking soda
6 eggs, separated
1½ cups all-purpose flour
1 teaspoon baking powder
½ teaspoon salt
¼ cup butter, melted and cooled
1 tablespoon sugar
2 cups fresh huckleberries or blueberries

In a small bowl, dissolve the baking soda in buttermilk. In a large bowl, lightly beat the egg yolks. Stir the buttermilk mixture into the egg yolks. Sift together the flour, baking powder, and salt and gently fold into the buttermilk mixture just enough to moisten. Gently fold in the melted butter and set aside. In a separate bowl, beat the egg whites until soft peaks form, then add the sugar and continue beating until stiff. Fold the egg whites gently into the batter and stir in the huckleberries. The batter should be a little bit lumpy.

Heat a griddle to medium-high, about 375 degrees. Lightly butter the hot griddle. Pour about ¼ cup of batter for each pancake. Cook until a few bubbles break on top of the pancake and the bottom is golden brown. Turn the pancake over and cook until bottom is golden brown.

Serves 6

1805 — The men work in the fields or at the benches,
at various trades; the women are occupied cooking food,
making pancakes and cakes, — NIEMCEWICZ

Rose Geranium Cake

*There are several varieties of culinary scented geraniums, the most popular being
the rose geranium. The flavor is not in the blossom, but in the leaves.
The role of scented geraniums in the garden and kitchen hail from an era when
exotic flavorings such as vanilla and lemon were costly and hard to come by.*

1½ cups all-purpose flour
⅔ cup sugar
2 teaspoons baking powder
½ teaspoon salt
⅓ cup butter, softened
⅔ cup milk
1 egg
6 rose geranium leaves

Icing:

2 tablespoons milk
1 teaspoon minced fresh
rose geranium leaves
⅔ cup powdered sugar

Preheat oven to 350 degrees. Butter and flour an 8-inch cake pan.

In a large bowl, sift together the flour, sugar, baking powder, and salt and make a
well in the center. Add the butter, milk, and egg to the well and beat until
smooth. Place the rose geranium leaves in the bottom of the prepared pan and
pour in the batter. Bake for about 30 minutes, or until a toothpick inserted in
the center comes out clean. Turn out onto a rack.

For the icing: Combine the milk with the minced rose geranium leaves and let
steep for 30 minutes. Strain the milk through a fine sieve into a bowl. Add the
powdered sugar and beat until smooth. Use to ice the cake while it is still warm
and let cool before serving.

Serves 6

MARCH 9, 1809 — *Th: Jefferson presents his respectful
salutations to mrs. Smith, and sends her the Geranium
she expressed a willingness to receive. it is in
very bad condition, having been neglected latterly, as not
intended to be removed. he cannot give it his parting
blessing more effectually than by consigning
it to the nourishing hand of mrs. Smith.*

— JEFFERSON to Mrs. Samuel Harrison Smith

Honey Cake with Almond Topping

Colonists brought their taste for honey and their honeybees when they first settled in North America. American beekeepers took great pride in the honey they produced, and because they never wasted anything, made elegant candles out of the beeswax that were highly prized over the more common tallow candles.

Almond Topping:
- ½ cup all-purpose flour
- ¼ cup packed brown sugar
- ¼ cup sugar
- ⅓ cup cold butter, cut into small pieces
- ½ cup chopped almonds

Honey Cake:
- ½ cup melted butter
- ½ cup honey
- 2 eggs
- ¼ cup sour cream
- 1 teaspoon vanilla extract
- ½ teaspoon almond extract
- 1½ cups all-purpose flour
- 1 teaspoon baking powder
- ½ teaspoon baking soda
- ½ teaspoon salt

Preheat oven to 350 degrees. Lightly oil an 8 by 8-inch baking dish.

For the topping: In a bowl, stir together the flour, brown sugar, and sugar with a fork until blended. Cut in the butter until the mixture resembles coarse meal. Stir in the almonds and set aside.

For the cake: In a large bowl, cream together the butter and honey. Add the eggs, one at a time, beating well after each addition. Stir in the sour cream, vanilla extract, and almond extract. Sift together the flour, baking powder, baking soda, and salt and stir into the creamed mixture until smooth. Pour the batter into the prepared baking dish and spoon on the reserved topping. Bake for about 35 to 40 minutes, or until a toothpick inserted in the center comes out clean.

JUNE 10, 1805 — *the bee martin or Kingbird is common to this country; tho' there are no bees in this country, nor have we met with a honey bee since we passed the entrance of the Osage River.* — LEWIS

Raspberry and Almond Coffee Cake

Coffee was first cultivated on the Arabian Peninsula during the 15th century, but didn't gain popularity in Europe or America until the 1700s. Like their modern counterparts, 18th century coffee shops were fashionable establishments to eat, meet, and discuss the issues of the day. Quick breads remain a popular accompaniment to a good cup of coffee.

Streusel:
- ⅓ cup all-purpose flour
- ¼ cup sugar
- ¼ cup butter
- ⅓ cup slivered almonds

- 1 cup fresh raspberries
- 4 ounces almond paste, chopped

Cake:
- 2 cups all-purpose flour
- 1 cup milk
- ¾ cup sugar
- ¼ cup butter, softened
- 1 egg
- 2 teaspoons baking powder
- 1½ teaspoons vanilla extract
- ½ teaspoon salt

Preheat oven to 350 degrees. Lightly oil a 9 by 9-inch baking dish.

For the streusel: In a bowl, stir together the flour and sugar. Cut in the butter until the mixture resembles coarse meal. Stir in the almonds and set aside.

For the cake: In a bowl, combine the flour, milk, sugar, butter, egg, baking powder, vanilla extract, and salt. Beat the ingredients for 3 minutes, scraping the sides of the bowl often. Pour half of the batter into the prepared baking dish and spread it out evenly. Sprinkle the raspberries over the batter. Sprinkle the almond paste over the raspberries. Pour the remaining cake batter on top. Sprinkle the streusel evenly over the batter. Bake for about 50 minutes, or until a toothpick inserted in the center comes out clean.

AUGUST 1, 1804 — *The Prarie which is situated below our Camp is above the high water leavel and rich covered with Grass from 5 to 8 feet high interspersed with copse of Hazel, Plumbs, Currents (like those of the U.S.) Rasberries & Grapes of Dift Kinds.* — CLARK

Cherry-Filled Butter Cookies

Wild cherry trees dotted much of the landscape through which Lewis and Clark led the Corps of Discovery. Higher in acid than sweet cherries, use sour cherry jam to more closely approximate the taste of wild cherries. These attractive cookies feature a dot of red cherry jam in their centers.

2 cups all-purpose flour	¾ cup butter, softened
⅔ cup sugar	1 egg
½ teaspoon baking powder	1 tablespoon vanilla extract
¼ teaspoon salt	½ cup sour cherry jam

Preheat oven to 350 degrees.

In a bowl, combine the flour, sugar, baking powder, and salt. Add the butter, egg, and vanilla extract and beat until you have a smooth dough. Divide dough into 4 portions. On a lightly floured surface, form each portion into a log about 12 inches long. Transfer the logs to 2 ungreased baking sheets and flatten the dough slightly to form rectangles. With your finger, make a depression down the center of each rectangle and fill with the cherry jam. Bake for 20 minutes. Remove from the oven and let cool slightly. Carefully transfer the rectangles to a cutting board. Cut the rectangles diagonally into 1-inch slices while still warm.

Makes about 60 cookies

1805 — *Not only are the houses surrounded by cherry trees but the roads are lined with cherry trees, some as big as the tallest oaks trees. They are wild black cherries rather than ordinary cherries; I have not seen those we call the morello anywhere. Whatever kind they may be, they provide both the travels and the local inhabitant with a good taste and with pleasant refreshment. For those riding by, it is enough to reach out in order to get a handful. Many birds, and almost as many boys and girls perch on the branches right up to the very top without picking the tree clean of this abundant and prolific fruit.* — NIEMCEWICZ

PLATE XVII

CHERRY

JUNE 25, 1805 — Great quanties of choke cherryes Goose berrys red & yallow berry, & red purple currents on the Edges of the water. we catch great quantities of Trout and a kind of muttel [mussel] flat backs and a Soft fish resembling Shad . . . the party amused themselves dancing untill 10 oClock all in cheerfulness and good humour. — ORDWAY

Molasses Ice Box Cookies

Jefferson had an icehouse built at Monticello to store the blocks of ice he cut and harvested from the rivers and lakes during the winter. A well-built icehouse would ensure a supply of ice into the following summer.

½ cup butter, softened
½ cup molasses
½ cup sugar
1 egg
2½ cups all-purpose flour
½ teaspoon ground cinnamon
½ teaspoon ground ginger
½ teaspoon salt
¼ teaspoon ground cloves
¼ teaspoon baking soda

Preheat oven to 375 degrees. Lightly oil 2 baking sheets.

In a small saucepan, stir together the butter and molasses over low heat until the butter has melted. Pour the molasses mixture into a large bowl. Add the sugar and beat until smooth. Add the egg and beat until smooth. Sift together the flour, cinnamon, ginger, salt, cloves, and baking soda. Beat the flour mixture into the creamed mixture until smooth. Divide the dough into 3 portions. Form into logs each about 10 inches long and wrap in plastic wrap. Chill in the refrigerator for 3 to 4 hours.

Slice each log crosswise into 24 rounds. Place on prepared baking sheets about 1 inch apart. Bake for 12 to 15 minutes or until golden brown.

Makes 72 cookies

JANUARY 24, 1810 — *The day before yesterday the mercury was at 5½° with us, a very uncommon degree of cold here. It gave us the first ice for the ice house.* — JEFFERSON to Joel Barlow

Gingersnaps

Believed to be good for ailments of the stomach, ginger had a respected place in the 18th century medicine cabinet. Combined with cinnamon and cloves, two other healing spices, gingersnaps just have to be good for you.

¾ cup butter, softened
1 cup packed brown sugar
¼ cup molasses
1 egg
2¼ cups all-purpose flour
2 teaspoons baking soda
1 teaspoon ground cinnamon
1 teaspoon ground ginger
½ teaspoon ground cloves
½ teaspoon salt
Sugar for rolling

Preheat oven to 375 degrees. Lightly grease 2 baking sheets.

In a large bowl, cream the butter, brown sugar, molasses, and egg until fluffy. Sift together the flour, baking soda, cinnamon, ginger, cloves, and salt and beat into the creamed mixture until smooth. Place the additional sugar in a shallow bowl. Roll the dough into balls the size of walnuts. Roll the balls in sugar and place 2 inches apart on the prepared baking sheets. Bake for 8 to 10 minutes. Remove from the oven and let cool on the baking sheet for 5 minutes before transferring to a rack to cool completely.

Makes about 48 cookies

FEBRUARY 11, 1805 — *...be pleased also to send these by the first safe boatman a hogshead of molasses. I say safe boatman because nothing is so liable to adulteration by them as molasses. The wine should also be confided to trustworthy hands...* — JEFFERSON

Hermits

Polite afternoon entertaining during the time of our third president Thomas Jefferson,
called for a pot of freshly brewed coffee and platters of sweet cookies.
These cookies use walnuts, a favorite nut combined with imported spices.
Of very old heritage, hermits are a traditional and satisfying cookie.

1	cup packed brown sugar
½	cup butter, softened
2	eggs
2	cups all-purpose flour
1½	teaspoons baking powder
1	teaspoon ground cinnamon
½	teaspoon salt
¼	teaspoon ground allspice
½	cup raisins
½	cup chopped walnuts

Preheat oven to 350 degrees. Lightly oil a baking sheet.

In a large bowl, cream the brown sugar and butter until smooth. Add the eggs and beat until smooth. In a small bowl, sift together the flour, baking powder, cinnamon, salt, and allspice and add to the creamed mixture. Beat until smooth. Stir in the raisins and walnuts. Drop by the tablespoonful onto the prepared baking sheet. Bake for about 10 to 12 minutes, or until lightly golden brown. Let cool on the baking sheet for 5 minutes before transferring to a rack to cool completely.

Makes about 36 cookies

SQUIRRELS

DECEMBER 23, 1805 — *I also gave a string of wompom to a chief, and sent a small piece of Sirimon to a sick Indian in the Town who had attached himself to me* — CLARK

OCTOBER 19, 1807 — I duly received your present of Sickel's pears, most of them in their highest point of perfection, two or three just past it. they exceeded anything I have tasted since I left France, & equalled any pear I had seen there. — JEFFERSON

Creams, Puddings & Pies

Vanilla Ice Cream Baked in Meringue

*Enjoyed by Thomas Jefferson and popularized in the 1860s by the famed
restaurant Delmonico's, this dessert ultimately became known as Baked Alaska.
The meringue provides an insulating blanket while baking, allowing the ice cream
to remain firm and frozen. Serve immediately so that guests may enjoy
the combination of hot meringue on top of cold ice cream. The cake should be
made a day ahead, because being slightly dry, it will absorb any of the
ice cream that may melt when baking.*

Cake:	Meringue:
3 eggs, separated	6 egg whites
⅛ teaspoon salt	⅛ teaspoon salt
½ cup sugar	1 cup sugar
¾ cup all-purpose flour	
1 quart vanilla ice cream	

Preheat oven to 375 degrees. Butter and flour a 9-inch round cake pan.

For the cake: In a bowl, beat the egg whites with the salt until they form soft peaks. Continue beating and gradually add the sugar a little at a time. Beat until stiff and glossy. Gently fold in the egg yolks. Sift the flour over the egg mixture and gently fold together, taking care not to deflate the mixture. Pour the batter into the prepared pan and bake for about 20 minutes, or until a toothpick inserted in the center comes out clean and the cake is golden brown. Remove from oven and cool for 5 minutes before turning out on a rack to cool completely. Cover with plastic wrap and let stand at room temperature overnight.

For the ice cream: Slightly soften the ice cream and press into an 8-inch diameter bowl that will hold 1 quart of ice cream. Place in the freezer and freeze for 1 hour. Briefly dip the bottom of the bowl in warm water to loosen the ice cream from the bowl. Unmold the ice cream onto a plate. Cover the ice cream with plastic wrap. Return the ice cream to the freezer and freeze overnight.

For the meringue: In a large bowl, beat the egg whites with the salt until they hold soft peaks. Add the sugar, a little at a time, beating constantly until the meringue holds stiff peaks.

Preheat oven to 450 degrees. Place a 12-inch round bottom of a spring-form pan on a baking sheet.

Working quickly, place the cake on the spring-form pan bottom. Transfer the ice cream on top of the cake. With a spatula, spread the meringue in a thick layer over the ice cream and cake and seal the meringue to the board. With the back of a spoon make decorative swirls in the meringue if desired. Bake for 5 to 7 minutes, or until the meringue is golden brown. Transfer the spring-form bottom to a platter and serve immediately.

Serves 8

FEBRUARY 6, 1802 — *Ice cream very good, crust wholly dried, crumbled into thin flakes; a dish somewhat like a pudding— inside white as milk or curd, very porous and light covered with cream sauce— very fine. Many other jimcracks, a great variety of fruit, plenty of wine and good.*
— SENATOR MANASSEH CUTLER of Massachusetts

French Vanilla Ice Cream

*A favorite of Thomas Jefferson, vanilla ice cream was a popular dessert at the
White House. If you haven't made an ice cream based on a custard before,
you will be pleasantly surprised at the creamy smoothness of this one. Easy to make,
this is a traditional, basic recipe on which other ultra-rich ice creams are based.*

2½ cups milk
¾ cup sugar
¼ cup heavy cream
1 vanilla bean, sliced in half lengthwise
6 egg yolks

In a heavy saucepan, combine the milk, sugar, cream, and vanilla bean. Bring the
mixture to a simmer over medium heat. Remove the saucepan from the heat
and let stand 5 minutes. Remove the vanilla bean. In a bowl, whisk the egg yolks
until smooth. Pour half of the hot milk mixture into the egg yolks, whisking constantly. Pour the egg yolk mixture back into the saucepan, whisking until smooth.
Bring the mixture to a simmer over medium-low heat, whisking constantly. The
mixture will thicken slightly and coat the back of a wooden spoon. Strain the
custard through a fine sieve into a bowl. Cover with plastic wrap and completely
chill the custard in the refrigerator. Pour the cold custard into an ice cream
maker and process according to the manufacturer's instructions.

Makes about 1 quart

JANUARY 3, 1809 — *if it is now as cold with you as it is here
I am in hopes you will be able & ready to fill the ice house.
it would be a real calamity should we not have ice to do it,
as it would require double the quantity of fresh meat in
summer had we not ice to keep it.* — JEFFERSON

Honey Ice Cream

Known as "the white man's fly," honeybees were not native to this continent,
yet they quickly integrated into the natural ecosystems, providing valuable
pollination for many native plants. This is an incredibly rich
and creamy ice cream, based on a cooked custard.

  3 cups milk
  1 cup heavy cream
  ½ cup honey
1½ teaspoons vanilla extract
  8 egg yolks
  ½ cup sugar

In a heavy saucepan, combine the milk, cream, honey, and vanilla extract. Bring the mixture to a simmer over medium heat. In a bowl, whisk together the egg yolks and sugar until smooth. Pour half of the hot milk mixture into the egg yolk mixture, whisking constantly. Pour the egg yolk mixture back into the saucepan, whisking until smooth. Bring to a simmer over medium-low heat, whisking constantly. The mixture will thicken slightly and coat the back of a wooden spoon. Strain the custard through a fine sieve into a bowl. Cover and completely chill the custard in the refrigerator. Pour the chilled custard into ice cream maker and process according to the manufacturer's instructions.

Makes about 1½ quarts

JANUARY 1797 — *After ten o'clock they play Washington's March;*
everybody goes to supper, or rather the ladies, and the gentlemen
eat the remains. The table is set with chocolate, coffee, tea,
cold meats, custards, etc. The ball continues afterwards up to
one o'clock in the morning. — NIEMCEWICZ

Pawpaw Ice Cream

Pawpaws have a flavor that can best be described as a creamy tropical custard. Hence their other name—custard apple. A favorite of the men of the Corps during their travels through Ohio, pawpaws grow wild in about twenty-five other states east of the Mississippi River. See Resources on page 151 for pawpaw products.

2 cups pawpaw purée, thawed if frozen
2 cups heavy cream
½ cup milk
1 cup sugar

Place the pawpaw purée in a bowl and set aside. In a heavy saucepan, stir together the cream, milk, and sugar. Bring the mixture to a simmer over medium heat. Slowly pour the cream mixture into the pawpaw purée, whisking to blend. Cover with plastic wrap and completely chill in the refrigerator. Pour the cold mixture into an ice cream maker and process according to the manufacturer's instructions.

Makes about 1½ quarts

SEPTEMBER 15, 1806 — *we landed one time only to let the men geather Pappaws or the custard apple of which this country abounds, and the men are very fond of.* — CLARK

PLATE XVIII

PLUM

AUGUST 30, 1806 ➝ we had not proceeded far before Saw a
large plumb orchd. of the most delicious plumbs, out of this
orchard 2 large Buck Elks ran the hunters killed them.
I stoped the canoes and brought in the flesh which was fat
and fine. Here the party collected as many plumbs as they could
eate and Several pecks of which they put by &c. ➝ CLARK

XVIII

Chocolate Pots de Crème

Chocolate pots de crème were a part of the Parisian cuisine enjoyed by Jefferson during his time as Ambassador to France. Simple to prepare, pots de crème are silky smooth ramekins filled with incredibly delicious chocolate custard. Observe the cooking time carefully and do not overbake.

½ cup sugar, divided
¼ cup cocoa powder
1⅔ cups milk, divided
4 egg yolks

Preheat oven to 350 degrees.

In a saucepan, stir together half of the sugar with the cocoa powder. Add 2 tablespoons of the milk to the cocoa mixture and whisk until completely blended. Slowly add the remaining milk in a thin stream, whisking constantly. Place the saucepan over medium heat and bring to a simmer.

In a bowl, whisk together the egg yolks with the remaining sugar until smooth. As soon as the milk mixture comes to a simmer, pour the hot milk mixture into the egg yolk mixture, whisking constantly. Pour the mixture into four 1-cup ramekins. Place the ramekins in a pan and add enough boiling water to the pan to come halfway up the sides of the ramekins. Bake for about 35 minutes, or until the custard has set but is still a little soft in the center. Remove the ramekins from the pan and cool to room temperature. Cover and chill for at least 3 hours before serving.

Serves 4

SEPTEMBER 13, 1806 — *I felt my self very unwell and derected a little Chocolate which Mr. McClellin gave us, prepared of which I drank about a pint and found great relief.* — LEWIS

Almond Blancmange with Strawberries

The origins of blancmange are unclear, but it is an extremely old and traditional European pudding. One of just a few family recipes in Jefferson's own handwriting to survive, blancmange transforms simple ingredients into elegant presentation. Leading chefs and restaurants across America are once again rediscovering the beauty of blancmange.

1	cup finely ground almonds
1¼	cups water
4	teaspoons powdered gelatin
⅓	cup cold water
1	cup sugar
1	teaspoon almond extract
1	cup milk
1	cup heavy cream
2	cups whole fresh strawberries

Lightly oil a 6-cup ring mold and wipe out the excess oil.

In a small bowl, stir together the ground almonds and 1¼ cups water. Let stand for 1 hour.

Place a colander in a large bowl. Lay a damp tea towel in the colander. Pour the almond mixture into the center of the towel, allowing the liquid to strain through into the bowl. Bring up the sides of the towel and twist around the almonds, squeezing out as much liquid as possible. Discard the almonds.

In a small bowl, soften the gelatin in the ⅓ cup water. Set aside.

In a saucepan, combine the almond liquid, sugar, and almond extract. Bring the mixture to a boil, then remove the saucepan from the heat and whisk in the softened gelatin. Pour the mixture into a large bowl and place it in a larger bowl of ice.

In the same saucepan, bring the milk to a boil over medium heat. Stir the scalded milk into the almond mixture. Continue to stir until completely cool.

Whip the cream until stiff, then gently fold into the cooled almond mixture. Pour into the prepared mold, cover with plastic wrap, and chill overnight.

To serve, dip the bottom of the mold in hot water for a moment to loosen the blancmange from the mold. Invert onto a serving plate and carefully remove the mold. Fill the center with the strawberries.

Serves 10

STRAWBERRIES

1802 — Dessert consists of an enormous quantity of confections, local fruit or fruit imported from the Islands. At times there is fresh sugar cane. I remember how making jellies and blanc mange kept my wife and me busy for several evenings. — NIEMCEWICZ

Steamed Maple Pudding with Caramelized Maple Sauce

Steamed puddings are moist and dense with flavor and nothing like the dainty, more fashionable confections favored by the European elite with whom Jefferson lived and worked while in France.

Steamed Maple Pudding:
- ½ cup butter, softened
- ½ cup sugar
- 1 cup maple syrup
- 1 teaspoon baking soda
- ½ cup buttermilk
- 3 eggs
- ¾ cup all-purpose flour
- ¼ teaspoon salt

Caramelized Maple Sauce:
- ¼ cup butter
- ¼ cup sugar
- ½ cup maple syrup
- ¼ cup heavy cream

Grease and flour a 5-cup pudding mold with a tight-fitting lid.

For the pudding: In a bowl, cream together the butter and sugar until fluffy. Beat in the syrup. In a small bowl, dissolve the baking soda in the buttermilk with a fork. Stir into the maple mixture. Add the eggs and beat until smooth. Add the flour and salt and beat until smooth. Pour the batter into the prepared pudding mold. Cover the mold tightly with the lid. Place the mold on a rack in a deep pot and add enough water to come halfway up the sides of the mold. Bring the water to a boil over high heat, reduce the heat to medium-low, and cover the pot. Steam the pudding for 2½ hours, checking occasionally to make sure that the water has not evaporated, adding more if needed. Remove the mold from the pot and remove the lid. Let cool for 15 minutes before turning out onto a serving plate.

For the caramelized maple sauce: In a saucepan, melt the butter over medium heat. Whisk in the sugar and bring to a boil over high heat. Cook, whisking constantly, until the mixture caramelizes and turns golden brown. Pour in the maple syrup and cream and bring to a boil. Remove the sauce from the heat and transfer to a sauceboat. Serve immediately with the steamed maple pudding.

Serves 8

JUNE 27, 1790 — Though large countries of our union are covered with the Sugar maple as heavily as can be conceived, and that this tree yields a sugar equal to the best from cane, yields it in great quantity, with no other labor than what the women & girls can bestow, who attend to the drawing off & boiling the liquor, & the trees when skillfully tapped will last a great number of years, yet the ease with which we had formerly got cane sugar, had prevented our attending to this resource. late difficulties in the sugar trade have excited attention to our sugar trees, and it seems fully believed by judicious persons, that we can not only supply our own demand, but make for exportation. — JEFFERSON

SUGAR MAPLE

Orange and Blueberry Pudding

*Steamed puddings were well-known in our great-grandmother's kitchens, but they
have fallen out of favor, perhaps due to the need to steam-cook them for two hours.
It is a pity, since they are easy to assemble and the moist texture and delicacy
of flavor cannot be equaled through other means.*

½ cup butter, softened
1 cup sugar
3 eggs
¼ cup freshly squeezed orange juice
1 tablespoon finely minced orange zest
1¼ cups all-purpose flour
2 teaspoons baking powder
1 cup fresh blueberries

Grease and flour a 5-cup pudding mold with a tight-fitting lid.

In a bowl, cream together the butter and sugar until fluffy. Add the eggs, one at
a time, beating well after each addition. Add the orange juice and orange zest
and beat until smooth. Add the flour and baking powder and beat until smooth.
Gently fold in the blueberries. Spoon the batter into the prepared pudding
mold. Cover the mold tightly with the lid. Place the mold on a rack in a deep pot
and add enough boiling water to come halfway up the sides of the mold. Bring
the water to a boil over high heat, reduce the heat to medium-low, and cover the
pot. Steam the pudding for 2 hours, checking occasionally to make sure that the
water has not evaporated and adding more if needed. Remove the mold from
the pot and remove the lid. Let cool for 15 minutes before turning out onto a
serving plate.

Serves 6 to 8

AUGUST 15, 1805 — *This morning I arose very early and as
hungary as a wolf. I had eat nothing yesterday except one scant
meal of the flour and berries except the dryed cakes of berries
which did not appear to satisfy my appetite as they appeared to
do those of my Indian friends. I found on enquiry of
Mc.Neal that we had only about two pounds of flour remaining.
This I directed him to divide into two equal parts and to cook*

the one half this morning in a kind of pudding with the burries as he had done yesterday and reserve the balance for the evening. on this new fashoned pudding four of us breakfasted, giving a pretty good allowance also to the Chief who declared it the best thing he had taisted for a long time. he took a little of the flour in his hand, taisted and examined [it] very scrutinously and asked me if we made it of roots. I explained to him the manner in which it grew. ⟶ LEWIS

ORANGE

Bread and Butter Pudding
with Cherries

*Bread and butter puddings are a delicious way to use up leftover bread.
Americans were resilient and resourceful and produced inventive dishes
that utilized every last scrap of available food. These skills stood the comrades
of the Corps of Discovery in good stead.*

1 loaf day-old French bread, cut into 1-inch cubes
2 cups cherry preserves
6 eggs
½ cup sugar
3 cups milk
1 teaspoon finely minced lemon zest
⅛ teaspoon freshly grated nutmeg
6 tablespoons butter, cut into small pieces

Preheat oven to 325 degrees. Butter a 3-quart baking dish.

Spread half of the bread cubes in the bottom of the prepared baking dish.
Spoon the cherry preserves evenly over the bread cubes. Top with the remaining
bread cubes. Set aside.

In a bowl, whisk together the eggs and sugar until well blended. Stir in the milk,
lemon zest, and nutmeg until smooth. Pour the mixture evenly over the top of
the bread cubes. Let stand 1 hour to allow the bread to absorb the milk mixture.
Dot with butter evenly over the top. Bake for 1 hour, or until golden brown.

Serves 10 to 12

MAY 12, 1805 — *it bears a fruit which much resembles the wild
cherry in form and colour tho' larger and better flavoured.
it's fruit ripens about the beginning of July and continues on
the trees untill the latter end of September. The Indians of
the Missouri make great use of this cherry which they prepare
for food in various ways, sometimes eating when first
plucked from the trees or in that state pounding them mashing
the seed boiling them with roots or meat, or with the prarie
beans and white apple;* — LEWIS

PLATE XIX

APPLE

JANUARY 22, 1788 — the barrels of Apples & Cranberries
can come by water only, as the motion of land carriage
would reduce them to mummy. — JEFFERSON

XIX

Tender Pie Crust

A food processor may be used quite expeditiously to cut in the butter, however to ensure a tender crust, do not overprocess or allow the butter to become warm.

2½   cups all-purpose flour
¼   cup sugar
½   teaspoon salt
1¼   cups cold butter, cut into small pieces
⅓   cup ice cold water

In a large bowl, combine the flour, sugar, and salt. Cut in the butter until the mixture resembles coarse meal. Stir the water into the flour mixture until the dough comes together and forms a ball. Form the dough into 2 balls and flatten into discs. The dough may be rolled out immediately on a lightly floured surface. Makes enough dough for one 10-inch double-crust pie.

SEPTEMBER 27TH, 1805 — *The river below the fork is about 200 yards wide; the water is clear as chrystal, from 2 to 5 feet deep... The bottom of the river is stony and the banks chiefly composed of a round hard species of stone.* — GASS

Dried Apple Pie

*Around 1800, three years before Lewis and Clark set off, John Chapman, a.k.a.
Johnny Appleseed, arrived in the Ohio River Valley establishing orchards and
spreading the gospel of the apple. This apple pie, with the apples rehydrated in apple
juice, is a real treat directly out of our founding fathers' time.*

1   pound dried apple slices
2   cups apple juice
2   cups water
1   cup sugar
¼   cup butter
1½   teaspoons ground cinnamon
     Sugar for sprinkling
     Pastry for a double-crust 10-inch pie, see page 135

Preheat oven to 450 degrees.

In a large saucepan, combine the dried apples, apple juice, and water. Bring to a
simmer over medium heat, then reduce the heat to medium-low, and simmer
until most of the liquid has been absorbed. Stir in the sugar, butter, and cinnamon and simmer until the mixture is thick.

Line a 10-inch pie plate with half the pastry dough and prick all over with a fork.
Pour the apple mixture into the pie shell and adjust the top crust. Cut decorative
vents in the top crust to allow the steam to escape. Sprinkle about 1 tablespoon
of sugar over the top of the pie. Bake for 10 minutes. Reduce the oven temperature to 350 degrees, and bake for an additional 40 minutes.

Serves 8

DECEMBER 24, 1804 — *Some snow fell this morning; about 10
it cleared up, and the weather became pleasant. This evening
we finished our fortification. Flour, dried apples,
pepper and other articles were distributed in the different
messes to enable them to celebrate Christmas in a proper
and social manner.* — GASS

Maple Sugar Pie

*Jefferson believed the United States could become self-sufficient in sugar production
by cultivating the sugar maple. Long before its use by European settlers,
Northeast Indians were enjoying this uniquely American sweetener.*

1 pound (2¾ cups) maple sugar
¼ cup all-purpose flour
¾ cup melted butter
3 eggs
¾ cup half-and-half

    One 10-inch unbaked pie shell

    French Vanilla Ice Cream, see page 124

Preheat oven to 350 degrees.

In a large bowl, combine the maple sugar and flour with a fork until blended.
Add the melted butter and beat until smooth. Add the eggs, one at a time, beating well after each addition. Add the half-and-half and beat for about 5 minutes,
or until the mixture is light and fluffy. Pour the maple sugar mixture into the unbaked pie shell and bake for about 50 minutes, or until the custard has almost
set but is still a little soft in the middle. The filling will continue to firm up as it
cools. Serve with French Vanilla Ice Cream.

Serves 8

FEBRUARY 20, 1804 — *The four men who are engaged in
making sugar will continue in that employment untill
further orders, and will receive each a half a gill of extra
whiskey pr day and be exempt from guard duty.* — LEWIS

Fried Peach Pies

Thomas Jefferson was so enamored with peaches that he planted as many different varieties as possible in his orchard at Monticello. In fact, Jefferson was a serious horticulturist who experimented with such modern farming practices as hybridization and crop rotation.

Filling:
- 1 pound fresh peaches, peeled and chopped
- ¼ cup sugar
- ¼ teaspoon ground cinnamon
- ¼ teaspoon vanilla extract

Pastry:
- 1½ cups all-purpose flour
- ½ teaspoon baking powder
- ½ teaspoon salt
- ½ cup cold butter, cut into small pieces
- 1 egg
- 2 tablespoons cold water

  Oil for deep frying

  Powdered sugar

For the filling: In a saucepan, combine the peaches, sugar, cinnamon, and vanilla. Simmer over medium-low heat until the peaches are reduced to a thick sauce. Set aside.

For the pastry: In a large bowl, stir together the flour, baking powder, and salt. Cut in the butter until the mixture resembles coarse meal. In a small bowl, whisk together the egg and water. Stir the egg mixture into the flour mixture until the dough forms a ball. Gather the dough into a ball, wrap it in plastic wrap, and flatten into a disc. Chill for about 30 minutes.

Turn the dough out onto a lightly floured surface and roll out to ¼-inch thick. Cut out rounds with a 4-inch cookie cutter. Place about 1½ teaspoons of the peach filling in the center of each round of dough. Dip a small pastry brush in water and moisten the edges of the dough. Fold the round in half and crimp the edges together with a fork.

Add oil to a deep fryer to a depth of 3 inches. Heat the oil to 385 degrees. Deep-fry the pies, a few at a time, until golden brown on both sides. Remove the pies with a slotted spoon and drain on paper towels. Sprinkle the pies with powdered sugar and serve.

Makes about 16 pies

FEBRUARY 25, 1807 ⟶ *I have sent some cuttings both of the pears and the stone-fruits... The Lady's favourite—a small yellow peach of exquisite flavour—a late importation from France— ripens full of juice.* ⟶ MATLAK TO JEFFERSON

Homemade Elk Mincemeat

This is a traditional and very old-fashioned classic Christmas pie.
The mincemeat itself should be made well in advance of the holiday season.
A pressure cooker is absolutely essential to safely preserve the mincemeat
through canning. If you lack one, the mincemeat may be frozen
and thawed.

1 pound elk stew meat or beef stew meat, finely diced
1½ cups water
½ pound suet, coarsely chopped
4 green apples, peeled, cored, and finely chopped
4 cups raisins
3 cups currants
2 cups golden raisins
2 cups sugar

1 cup brandy
½ cup candied citron, finely chopped
Juice of 1 lemon
Zest of 1 lemon, finely minced
Juice of 1 orange
Zest of 1 orange, finely minced
1½ teaspoons salt
½ teaspoon ground nutmeg
½ teaspoon ground mace

In a saucepan, combine the elk meat and the water. Cover and simmer over low heat for 3 hours. Put the suet in the bowl of a food processor and process until finely ground. In a large pot, stir together the cooked elk, suet, apples, raisins, currants, golden raisins, sugar, brandy, citron, lemon juice, lemon zest, orange juice, orange zest, salt, nutmeg, and mace. Cover and simmer over medium-low heat for 1½ hours.

Immediately ladle the mincemeat into hot, sterilized quart jars, leaving a 1-inch headspace. Wipe the rims of the jars and adjust the lids. Process in a dial-gauge pressure canner at 11 pounds pressure for 90 minutes if your altitude is 0–2000 feet; or 12 pounds pressure for 90 minutes if your altitude is 2001–4000 feet; or 13 pounds pressure for 90 minutes if your altitude is 4001–6000 feet; or 14 pounds of pressure for 90 minutes if your altitude is 6001–8000 feet.

Makes 3 quarts

DECEMBER 25, 1805 — at day light this morning we we[re] awoke by the discharge of the fire arm[s] of all our party & a Salute, Shouts and a Song which the whole party joined in under our windows, after which they retired to their rooms were chearfull all the morning... The day proved Showerey wet and disagreeable we would have Spent this day the nativity of Christ in feasting, had we any thing either to raise our Sperits or even gratify our appetites, our Diner concisted of pore Elk, so much Spoiled that we eate it thro' mear necessity, Some spoiled pounded fish and a fiew roots. — CLARK

Mocha Cream Pie

*Yet another epicurean gift from the New World, chocolate was brought to Europe by
the Spanish explorers from Central America. The word chocolate is derived
from the Indian word* chocolatl. *Slow to catch on at first, once it was sweetened,
the popularity of chocolate exploded during the latter part of the 16th century
and has never waned to this day.*

2 cups milk
1 cup sugar, divided
2 ounces unsweetened chocolate
4 egg yolks
¼ cup cornstarch
¼ cup strong coffee
2 tablespoons butter
½ teaspoon vanilla extract

1 pre-baked 10-inch pie shell

In a heavy saucepan, combine the milk, half of the sugar, and chocolate. Bring
the mixture to a simmer over medium heat. In a bowl, whisk the egg yolks, remaining sugar, cornstarch, and coffee until smooth. Pour half of the hot milk
mixture into the egg yolks, whisking constantly. Pour the egg yolk mixture back
into the saucepan, whisking until smooth. Bring the mixture to a simmer over
medium heat, whisking constantly until it thickens to the consistency of pudding. Remove the saucepan from the heat and whisk in the butter and vanilla.
Pour the filling into the baked pie crust. Chill thoroughly before serving.

Serves 8

JUNE 25, 1805 — *I had a little coffee for breakfast
which was to me a necessity as I had not tasted any
since last winter.* — CLARK

PLATE XX

FERRET, WEASEL, ERMINE, SABLE, MARTIN, POLE CAT, AND SKUNK

AUGUST 20, 1805 — the ermin which[h] is known to the traiders of the N.W. by the name of the white weasel is the genuine ermine, — LEWIS

Pumpkin Pie

*From the beautiful orange fruit lying heavily in pumpkin patches to the fragrance
of pumpkin pie during the holidays, we associate pumpkins with bountiful harvests,
family unity, and all that is special about America. Yet for three years,
Lewis and Clark did without those comforts, sacrificing warmth and ease for the
chance to explore this great land. Enjoy this special pie next holiday and
give thanks for the tremendous generosity of this country.*

 2 cups packed brown sugar
 2 cups pumpkin purée
 4 eggs, lightly beaten
 2 teaspoons ground cinnamon
 1 teaspoon ground ginger
1¾ cups milk, warmed

    One 10-inch unbaked pie shell

Preheat oven to 450 degrees.

In a large bowl, whisk together the brown sugar, pumpkin purée, eggs, cinnamon, and ginger until smooth. Whisk in the milk until smooth. Pour the filling into the unbaked pie shell. Bake for 10 minutes, then reduce the temperature to 325 degrees and continue to bake for an additional 40 minutes.

APRIL 3, 1814 — *Th: J. presents his compliments to
mr Geltson and his thanks for the pumpkin seed he has
been so kind as to send him.* — JEFFERSON to David Gelston

Raspberry and Almond Tart

Wild berries were among the few sweet foods enjoyed by the Native Americans—having neither honey nor sugar (other than maple sugar in the Northeast), berries were an eagerly awaited treat each summer and fall. Enjoy this elegant and refined treat made entirely with ingredients familiar to Lewis, Clark, and Jefferson.

Sweet Pastry Dough:
- 1⅓ cups all-purpose flour
- 3 tablespoons sugar
- ¼ teaspoon salt
- ½ cup cold butter, cut into small pieces
- 1 egg
- 2 tablespoons cold water
- 1 teaspoon vanilla extract

Filling:
- 4 eggs
- ⅓ cup sugar
- 6 ounces almond paste
- ½ cup all-purpose flour
- ¾ cup raspberry jam
- ½ cup slivered almonds

Preheat oven to 350 degrees.

For the sweet pastry dough: In a large bowl, stir together the flour, sugar, and salt. Cut in the butter until the mixture resembles coarse meal. In a small bowl, whisk together the egg, water, and vanilla. Stir the egg mixture into the flour mixture until the dough forms a ball. Gather the dough into a ball, wrap it in plastic wrap, and flatten into a disc. Chill for about 30 minutes.

Turn dough out onto a lightly floured surface and roll out to fit a 10-inch tart pan with a removable bottom.

For the filling: In a bowl, beat together the eggs and sugar until foamy. Crumble the almond paste and beat into the egg mixture. Add the flour and beat until well mixed.

Spread the raspberry jam over the bottom of the crust. Spread the almond paste mixture evenly over the jam. Sprinkle the slivered almonds on top. Bake for 35 to 40 minutes, or until golden. Cool completely before removing the tart from the pan.

Serves 12

RASPBERRIES

FEBRUARY 11, 1806 — *the stem is armed with sharp and hooked bryors. The leaf is petiolate, ternate and resembles in shape and appearance that of the purple Raspberry common to the atlantic states. The frute is a berry resembling the Blackberry in every respect and is eaten when ripe and much esteemed by the natives* — CLARK

Squash Custard Pie

The Mandan Indians of what is now North Dakota, with whom Lewis and Clark spent their first winter, graciously shared their foodstuffs with the explorers, including squash, corn, and beans. This squash custard pie, similar to pumpkin pie, can be made with any of the winter squashes, but is especially beautiful when made with the golden-yellow acorn squash.

2 acorn squashes
1 cup sugar
4 eggs
½ cup heavy cream
1 teaspoon ground ginger

   One unbaked 10-inch pie shell

Preheat oven to 375 degrees. Lightly oil a baking sheet.

Cut the squash in half and place, cut-side down, on the prepared baking sheet. Bake for about 45 minutes, or until very tender. When the squash is cool enough to handle, scoop out the meat and mash until smooth. Measure out 2½ cups of mashed squash and set aside.

In a large bowl, whisk together the sugar and the eggs until smooth. Stir in the reserved squash until smooth. Stir in the cream and ginger until well blended. Pour the filling into the unbaked pie shell. Bake for about 1 hour, or until the pie is nearly set but still moves slightly in the middle. Let cool to room temperature before serving.

Serves 8

AUGUST 22, 1805 — *I gave him a few dryed squashes which we had brought from the Mandans he had them boiled and declared them to be the best thing he had ever tasted except sugar, a small lump of which it seems his sister Sah-cah-gar Wea had given him.* — LEWIS

Bibliography

Allgemeines Illustriertes Kochbuch. Compiled by the Deutschen Hausfrauen et.al. Berlin: Peter J. Oestergaard, 1904

Ambrose, Stephen E. *Undaunted Courage: Meriwether Lewis, Thomas Jefferson, and the Opening of the American West.* New York: Touchstone, 1997

An American Lady. *The American Home Cook Book.* New York: Dick and Fitzgerald, 1854. Reprinted by Pryor Publications, Yorkletts, Whitstable, Kent, England: 1999

Anon. *Pennsylvania Dutch Cook Book of Fine Old Recipes.* Reading, PA: Culinary Arts Press, 1960

The American Heritage Cookbook and Illustrated History of American Eating & Drinking. Edited by the American Heritage Editors. New York: American Heritage Publishing Co., 1964

American Philosophical Society. *Benjamin Franklin: On the Art of Eating.* Princeton MA: Princeton University Press (paperbound), 1958

Anderson, Jean. *Recipes from America's Restored Villages.* New York: Doubleday & Company, Inc., 1975

Aresty, Esther B. *The Delectable Past.* 2nd ed. New York: Simon and Schuster, 1964

Bakeless, John. *Lewis and Clark Partners in Discovery.* New York: William Morrow and Co., 1947

Beecher, Catherine E. *Miss Beecher's Domestic Receipt-Book.* New York: Harper & Brothers, 1858. Reprinted by Dover Publications, Mineola, NY: 2001

Beilenson, Evelyn. *Early American Cooking.* White Plains, NY: Peter Pauper Press, 1985

Berolzheimer, Ruth. *American Woman's Cook Book.* New York: Butterick Publishing Co., 1947

Better Homes and Gardens, *Heritage Cook Book.* Des Moines, IA: Meredith Corporation, 1975

Betts, Edwin Morris, annot. *Thomas Jefferson's Garden Book 1766-1824; with Relevant Extracts from his Other Writing.* Philadelphia: American Philosophical Society, 1944

Betts, Edwin Morris, annot. *Thomas Jefferson's Farm Book 1774-1826; with Relevant Extracts from his Other Writing.* Philadelphia: American Philosophical Society, 1944. Reprinted by the University Press of Virginia, 1987

Bowen, Catherine Drinker. *John Adams and the American Revolution.* Boston: Little Brown and Co., 1950

Bonnefoit, Guy. *Unsere Weine Unsere Küche.* Mainz: Deutsches Weininstitut, 1989

Booth, Letha. *The Williamsburg Cookbook.* Williamsburg, VA: The Colonial Williamsburg Foundation, 1973

Brown, Alice Cooke. *Early American Herb Recipes.* Rutland, VT: Charles E. Tuttle, 1966

Brown, Dale. *American Cooking.* Foods of the World (Series) New York: Time-Life Books, 1968

Bryan, Lettice. *The Kentucky Housewife*. Cincinnati, OH, 1839. Reprinted by Applewood Books, Bedford, MA: 1985

Bullock, Helen D. *The Williamsburg Art of Cookery*. Williamsburg, VA: Colonial Williamsburg, 1966

Bullock, Helen D. compiled by; *Mary and Vincent Price Present A National Treasury of Cookery Recipes of Ante Bellum America*. Hamlin, NY: Heirloom Publishing Co., 1967

Burroughs, Raymond Darwin. *The Natural History of the Lewis and Clark Expedition*. Michigan State University Press, 1995

Cannon, Poppy and Patricia Brooks. *The President's Cookbook*. Funk & Wagnalls, 1968

Carter, Susannah. *The Frugal Housewife*. Boston: Houghton Mifflin, 1969

Catlin, George. *The North American Indians*. 2 Vol. Edinburgh: John Grant., 1903. Reprinted by Digital Scanning, Scituate, MA: 2000

Child, [Maria]. *The American Frugal Housewife*. Boston: Carter, Hendee, and Co., 1832. Reprinted by Chapman Billies, Sandwich, MA: 1999

De Voto, Bernard, ed. *The Journals of Lewis and Clark*. Boston: Houghton Mifflin, 1953

Donavan, Mary and Amy Hatrak, Frances Mills, Elizabeth Shull. *The Thirteen Colonies Cookbook*. Montclair, NJ: Montclair Historical Society, 1982

Earle, Alice Morse. *Home Life in Colonial Days*. New York: Grosset & Dunlap, 1898. Reprinted by The Berkshire Traveller Press, Stockbridge, MS: 1974

Ehrhardt, Mathilde. *Grosses Illustriertes Kochbuch*. Berlin: Verlagsdruckerei Merkur, 1902

Farmer, Fannie Merrit. *The Boston Cooking-School Cook Book*. Boston: 1896

Farmer's Almanac Cookbook. Edited by Clarissa M. Silitch. Dublin, NH: Yankee Books, 1982

Farrington, Doris E. *Fireside Cooks & Black Kettle Recipes*. Indianapolis/New York: Bobbs-Merrill Co., 1976

Feibleman, Peter S. *American Cooking: Creole and Acadian*. Foods of the World (series). New York: Time-Life Books, 1971

Fisher, Marian Cole. *Twenty Lessons in Domestic Science*. Calumet Baking Powder Company, St. Paul, MN: 1916

Floyd, Mark. "Lewis and Clark: planning a two-year dinner party for 45." Corvallis, OR: *OSU News*. 8/28/2001

Foxfire Book, The. Compiled and edited by the students of Rabun Gap-Nacoochee School under the direction of their teacher Eliot Wigginton. New York: Anchor Press/Doubleday, 1972

Freeman, Jefferson Davis. *Confederate Receipt Book: A Compilation of Over One Hundred Receipts Adapted to The Times*. Harriman, TN: Pioneer Press, 2000

Frost, Heloise. *Early American Recipes*. Newton, MA: Phillips Publishers, 1953

Given, Meta. *Modern Encyclopedia of Cooking*. Chicago IL: J.G. Ferguson and Associates, 1955

Glasse, Hannah. *The Art of Cookery Made Plain and Easy*. Alexandria, VA: Cotton & Stewart, 1805. Introduction by Karen Hess, reprinted by Applewood Books, Bedford, MA: 1997

Goodrich, S.G. *A Pictorial History of America*. Hartford, CN: House & Brown, 1847

Goodrich, S.G. *Johnson's Natural History*. 2 vols. Henry G. Allen & Co., 1894

Haedrich, Ken. *The Maple Syrup Cookbook.* Pownal, VT: Garden Way Publishing, 1989

Herter, George Leonard and Berthe R. Herter. *Bull Cook and Authentic Historical Recipes and Practices.* Waseca, MN: Herter's, 1962

Hess, John L. and Karen Hess. *The Taste of America.* New York: Grossman Publishers, 1977

Hess, Karen. *Martha Washington's Booke of Cookery.* New York: Columbia University Press, 1981

Hirtzler, Victor. *The Hotel St. Francis Cook Book.* San Francisco: The Hotel Monthly Press, 1919

Holland, Leandra. "Preserving Food on the L&C Expedition." *We Proceeded On.* August 2001

Grossman, Anne and Lisa Thomas. *Lobscouse and Spotted Dog.* New York: Norton, 1997

Holm, Don. "There Were No Supermarkets." *Northwest Magazine.* January 21, 1968

Holm, Don and Myrtle Holm. *Don Holm's Book of Food Drying, Pickling and Smoke Curing.* Caldwell, ID: The Caxton Printers, 1981

Home Cook Book, The. Compiled by the Ladies of Toronto and other Cities and Towns in Canada. Toronto: Rose-Belford Publishing Co., 1877

Kalm, Peter. *Travels in North America.* Revised and Edited by A. B. Chapman, 2 Vols. Mineola, NY: Dover Publications, 1964

Kimball, Marie. *Thomas Jefferson's Cook Book.* Charlottesville, VA: The University Press of Virginia, 1987

Klapthor, Margaret Brown, ed. *The First Ladies Cook Book: Favorite Recipes of All Presidents of the United States.* New York: Parent's Magazine Press, 1969

Leonard, Jonathan Norton. *American Cooking: New England.* Foods of the World (series). New York: Time-Life Books, 1971

Lesem, Jeanne. *The Pleasures of Preserving and Pickling.* Westminster, MD: Vintage Books, 1982

Leslie, Eliza. *Miss Leslie's Directions for Cookery.* Philadelphia: Henry Carey Baird, 1851. Reprinted by Dover Publications, New York 1999

Leslie, M. and J. Ordway. *The Journals of Captain Meriwether Lewis and Sergeant John Ordway.* Edited by Milo M. Quaife. The State Historical Society of Wisconsin, 1965

Lynn, Kristie and Richard W. Pelton. *The Early American Cookbook.* Deerfield Beach, FL: Liberty Publishing Co., 1991

Gass, Patrick. *The Journals of Patrick Gass.* 2 vol. Edited and annotated by Carol Lynn MacGregor. Missoula, MT: Mountain Press Publishing Co. 1997

McGee, Harold. *On Food and Cooking.* New York: Charles Scribner's Sons, 1984

McKendry, Maxime. *Seven Hundred Years of English Cooking.* New York: Exeter Books, 1973

Migliario, Allard, Titus, Nunemaker. *The Household Searchlight Recipe Book.* The Household Magazine, 1941

Neil, Marion Harris. *A Calender of Dinners.* Cincinnati, OH: The Procter & Gamble Co., 1925

Niemcewicz, Julian. *Under Their Vine and Fig Tree.* Trans. and ed. Metchie Budka, Elizabeth, NJ: The Grassmann Publishing Co., 1965

Parloa, Maria. *Miss Parloa's Kitchen Companion.* Boston: Dana Estes and Co., 1887

Perl, Lila. *Hunter's Stew and Hangtown Fry.* New York: The Seabury Press, 1977

Pierce, Anne. *Home Canning for Victory.* New York: Barrows and Co., 1942

Plymouth Antiquarian Society, *The Plimoth Colony Cook Book.* Plymouth Antiquarian Society, 1964

Prescott, Della R. *A Day In a Colonial Home.* Boston: Marshall Jones Co., 1921

Randolph, Mary. *The Virginia Housewife.* Philadelphia: Plaskitt, & Cugle, 1828. Reprinted by Oxmoor House, Birmingham, AL: 1984

Randolph, Sarah. *The Domestic Life of Thomas Jefferson.* New York: Frederick Ungar Publishing, 1976

Rorer, S[arah] T. *Philadelphia Cook Book: A Manual of Home Economics.* Philadelphia: Arnold and Co., 1914

Schweid, Richard. *Hot Peppers.* Berkeley, CA: Ten Speed Press, 1989

Simmons, Amelia. *American Cookery.* Hartford, CN: Hudson and Goodwin, 1796

Simmons, Amelia. *The First American Cookbook.* Facsimile of *American Cookery.* New York: Oxford University Press, 1958. Reprinted by Dover Publications, Mineola, NY: 1984.

Singleton, Esther. *The Story of the White House.* New York: The McClure Co., 1907

Sleight, Jack and Raymond Hull. *Home Book of Smoke-Cooking Meat, Fish & Game.* Mechanicsburg, PA: Stackpole Books, 1982

Smith, Eliza. *The Compleat Housewife.* Hitch & Hawes 1758. Reprinted by Studio Editions, Albuquerque, NM: 1994

Smith, Margaret B. *The First Forty Years of Washington Society.* New York: Scribner and Sons, 1906. Reprinted by Frederick Ungar Publishing, New York: 1965

Soyer, Alexis. *A Shilling Cookery for the People.* London: Routledge, Warne, and Routledge, 1860. Reprinted by Pryor Publications, Kent, England: 1999

Sparks, Elizabeth Hedgecock. *North Carolina and Old Salem Cookery.* Kernersville, NC: Kingsport Press, 1980

Staebler, Edna. *Food that Really Schmecks.* New York: McGraw-Hill Ryerson, 1968

Thwaites, Reuben Gold. *Original Journals of the Lewis and Clark Expedition.* 8 Vol. Dodd Mead & Co., 1904. Reprinted by Digital Scanning, Inc. Scituate, MA: 2001

Trager, James. *The Food Chronology.* New York: Henry Holt & Co., 1995

Tyree, Marion Cabell. *Housekeeping in Old Virginia.* Louisville, KY: John P. Morton & Co., 1879. Reprinted by Favorite Recipes Press, Louisville, KY: 1965

Walter, Eugene. *American Cooking: Southern Style.* Foods of the World (series) New York: Time-Life Books, 1971

Whelen, Jack. *Smoking Salmon & Trout.* Deep Bay, BC: Aerie Publishing, 1988

Whipple, Leslie. *The Oregon Trail Cookbook.* Bend, OR: Maverick Publications, 1992

Whitehill, Jane. *Food, Drink, and Recipes of Early New England.* Meriden, CN: Meriden Gravure Co., 1970

Wilstach, Paul. *Jefferson and Monticello.* Garden City, NY: Doubleday, Page & Co., 1925

Ziedrich, Linda. *The Joy of Pickling.* Boston: Harvard Common Press, 1998

Ziegler, Thos. P. *The Meat We Eat.* Danville IL: The Interstate Printers and Publishers, 1952

Resources

Earthy Delights, 1161 East Clark Road, Suite 260 DeWitt, MI 48820
1-800-367-4709 www.earthy.com
> From caviar and fois gras to freshly picked wild mushrooms and fiddlehead ferns, Earthy Delights sources the finest gourmet foods available.

Integration Acres, 160 Cherry Ridge Road, Albany, OH 45710
1-740-698-2124 www.integrationacres.com
> Integration Acres specializes in the pawpaw. Fresh pawpaws are shipped in the fall, while frozen pawpaw puree is available year-round.

Labot & Graham, 7855 McCracken Pike, Versailles, KT 40383
1-859-879-1812 www.woodfordreserve.com
> Woodford's was carried by the Corps of Discovery across North America. Labrot & Graham was the first distillery to make sour-mash whiskey, the first to use charred oak barrels for aging, and is now the only distillery to still use copper pot stills.

Lodge Manufacturing Company, PO Box 380, South Pittsburg, TN 37380
1-423-837-7181 www.lodgemgf.com
> In business for over one hundred years, Lodge Manufacturing is the last American producer of cast-iron cookware. Their flat-topped Dutch oven was originally developed by Paul Revere.

Luhr-Jensen & Sons, PO Box 297, Hood River, OR 97031
1-800-366-3811 www.luhrjensen.com
> Luhr-Jensen & Sons is one of the nation's largest manufacturers of fishing lures and baits. They have developed a line of small, easy-to-use food smokers, wood chips, brines, seasonings, and sausage kits.

Maverick Ranch Natural Meats, 5360 North Franklin Street, Denver, CO 80216
1-800-49RANCH www.maverickranch.com
> Owned and operated by the Moore family, Maverick beef is guaranteed free from antibiotics, steroids, and pesticides.

Morse Farms, 1169 County Road, Montpelier VT 05602
1-800-242-2740 www.morsefarm.com
> The Morse family has been tapping maple trees in Vermont since 1782. Today, in addition to selling out of their farm store in Montpelier, they ship worldwide.

Nicky USA, Inc., 223 South East 3rd Avenue, Portland, OR 97214
1-800-469-4162 www.nickyusawildgame.com
Nicky USA specializes in nationwide distribution of Scottish game, Argentine beef, fois gras, and free-range, antibiotic- and hormone-free, Oregon grown lamb.

Prairie Harvest, 350 Hillsview Drive, Spearfish, SD 57783
1-605-642-5676 www.prairieharvest.com
Steve Hauff, a pioneer in the sales of wild game, has sold to leading restaurants since 1983. Located near the historic Black Hills of South Dakota.

Robinson-Ransbottom Pottery, 5545 Third Street, Roseville, OH 43777
1-740-697-7355 www.rrpco.com
A producer of traditional pickling crocks, Robinson-Ransbottom traces its origins to the pre-Civil War pottery industry in Ohio.

Seattle's Finest Exotic Meats, 17532 Aurora Avenue North, Shoreline, WA 98133
1-800-680-4375 www.exoticmeats.com
Founded in 1992, Seattle's Finest Exotic Meats offers over 32 different varieties of low-fat, low-cholesterol, and premium quality exotic meats.

The Smithfield Collection, PO Box 487, Smithfield, VA 23430
1-800-628-2242 www.smithfieldcollection.com
The Smithfield Collection traces its history back to 1779 and is the oldest meat packer in the United States.

St. George Spirits, 2900 Main Street, Alameda, CA 94501
1-510-658-7934 www.stgeorgespirits.com
Founded in 1982 by Jorg Rupf, St. George Spirits pioneered the distillation of clear fruit eau de vie in America.

Sugarwoods Farm, 1122 Still Hill Glover, VT 05839
1-800-245-3718 www.sugarwoodsfarm.com
Sugarwoods farm specializes in the production of maple sugar and syrup for restaurants and food producers as well as consumers.

Sunnyland Farms Inc., Willson Road at Pecan City, Albany, GA 31706
1-800-999-2488 www.sunnylandfarms.com
Since 1948, Jane and Harry Willson have been filling orders for their superb pecans, dried fruits, candies, and fruitcakes.

Index

*The handwritten font used for the quotes
in the text of this book was created from the
handwriting of Thomas Jefferson.*

*The type used for the text is New Baskerville,
a type face originally designed in
the eighteenth century by John Baskerville
and digitized for modern use.*

The display type is Caslon Antigua.